"We must look to the land with a deeper understanding because the land is life and to destroy the land limits life."

George Laycock, one of America's best-known naturalists, has written this shocking indictment of the corporations, politicians, and government agencies who, for short-term gain, have ravaged our nation's landscape and threatened the well-being of every American.

The Diligent Destroyers is not a purely emotional plea, but a closely reasoned, carefully documented account of the billions of dollars squandered, the recreational opportunities lost forever, and the wealth of natural resources totally destroyed by the dam-builders, the strip miners, the highway engineers, and their self-serving allies.

But most important, this book offers solutions: a sound, practical program every concerned citizen can support to bring an end to this irrevocable destruction of our land's wealth.

More Ballantine Books
You Will Enjoy

THE DILIGENT DESTROYERS

GEORGE LAYCOCK

AN AUDUBON/BALLANTINE BOOK

An Intext Publisher

NATIONAL AUDUBON SOCIETY
1130 Fifth Avenue, New York, N.Y. 10028

BALLANTINE BOOKS, INC.
101 Fifth Avenue, New York, N.Y. 10003

Contents

Man and His World

Yesterday we used stones for tools. Today, with millions of others, I sit, fascinated, watching the television screen as billowing yellow flames sear the sands of Cape Kennedy with a force that propels astronauts and their capsules into space. Man's genius has taken the raw materials of a wilderness environment and converted them totally to his own uses within a few hundred years.

Out of our accomplishments have grown our comfort and satisfaction. No longer do we have to be cold because it is cold around us, or hot because the sun shines. We have machines to transport us in comfort, do our chores, entertain us, and lift us in our daily activities up and above the harsh elements of our environment. And we would not trade the accomplishments of our tools and the knowledge we have today for any age that came before. We would not give back our modern highways for the mud roads that preceded them. We would not willingly sacrifice the comforts brought us by electric power whether it is generated beneath giant dams, or from the burning of strip mined coal.

This sheer comfort we have created for ourselves dulls the warning that we have gone too far in manipulating the elements of our environment—too far for our own long-range good. We pollute the air we must breathe, the water we must drink, and the foods we must consume. And we also pollute the landscape with our works. Rare indeed is the corner of the earth that has not yet felt the bite of man's tools. We send great shovels to disfigure the tops of the mountains. We dispatch our highway engineers, with their rumbling bulldozers, into the virgin woodlands and quiet parks. We dig and claw into those cradles of life, the estuaries.

We call it enterprise when men tear down the mountains for coal, and we speak of progress as we waste money on great canals of little true worth. We erase the pristine and replace the wilderness with masterpieces of our own design.

We take pride in the great reservoirs that provide water to carry our detergents and flush our baby-blue commodes. We take pride in magnificent highways which connect our neon jungles and concrete ghettos. For too long, gripped in a technological mentality, we have seen only the good in what we create and lost sight of the values we destroy. The engineer has become our king, and technology, which should be the tool, has become the master.

The engineer believes in his mission with a singleness of purpose that is impressive, and a narrowness that is frightening. But he cannot alone be blamed: we have created the atmosphere that condones such thinking.

Already, we have passed that point in human population where the good life is assured us. As a species we have learned how to keep each other alive and extend the life expectancy of the individual. But we have failed to deal with the birth rate. As population levels pass the bearable, there is strife, rioting, hunger, and uncertainty about the future. In a time of growing need for space, solitude, and relief from stress, we continue the destruction of the earth's natural areas.

Many of our mistakes can still be corrected. The junkyards and billboards can be moved. The electric wires draping the countryside can, as our technology improves, be buried out of sight. Even the pollution of the lakes and rivers—given time enough and money enough—can be cured and the waters restored. The air can be cleaned of the filth that floats there.

But many injuries inflicted on our environment are sores that cannot be cured—even if someday we seek to correct the mistakes. Highways, once in the wrong places, are not taken up. Valleys flooded beneath giant reservoirs are flooded for all foreseeable time. Estuaries ruined, may be beyond reclamation, and mountains the strip miners disfigure are beyond hope. Such irreversible changes are the subject of this book.

In the pages that follow, the Army Corps of Engineers, as our major water management agency, is examined at some length. Close behind comes the Bureau of Reclamation whose efforts are restricted largely to western states. The strip miners and shell dredgers are regional or local menaces. The highway engineers are everywhere.

We are occasionally assured that some of these agencies are losing their old arrogant approach to the landscape, and those who take exception to their works. We are told that the Corps of Engineers is changing its stripes, that there is an awakening ecological conscience. At the top level there is refreshing evidence that this may be true. But examination of the annual budget requests for Corps projects reveals no cutback in the rush to remodel America.

Instead of slowing down these attacks on the landscape, we have accelerated them. As the works of man spread into even the remote corners of the land, the sacrifice of each remaining natural area assumes a growing importance. It is frightening to contemplate . that, even today, we permit those agencies that build dams and highways to proceed, largely on their own, with no truly effective over-all planning.

As long as we permit the builders, diggers, and destroyers to go their way essentially uncontrolled—as they do today—we share the blame for the loss of increasingly vital portions of the abundant land which was our heritage.

George Laycock
February, 1969

"A clear stream, a long horizon, a forest wilderness and open sky—these are man's most ancient possessions. In a modern society, they are his most priceless."

Lyndon B. Johnson
Message to the 90th Congress

PART I

"The Corps is now working toward the maximum development of our rivers."

U. S. Army Corps of Engineers

1. The Dam Builders

For fifteen miles the North Fork of the shallow Red River tumbles down through giant hardwoods in the Daniel Boone National Forest in eastern Kentucky. The little stream dominates a rocky glen where it has spent sixty million years carving its path to a depth of six hundred feet. Its waters wash the base of palisades and flow through a wild garden, unique in the eastern half of the United States.

The foot trail winding along the creek into the heart of the gorge through the deep forests, leads to a shaded and scenic retreat where elusive wild turkeys prosper and white-tailed deer live. Hemlocks grow in the deep-shaded glens, and tangled thickets of rhododendron flank the trail. This deep valley, some fifty miles east of Lexington, where time and water have carved the rocks, is a wonderland of rare natural bridges and stone arches.

On a November day in 1967, five hundred citizens assembled in this valley to stage a wilderness protest march against the plans of the U. S. Army Corps of Engineers. At the head of the protest was Supreme Court Justice William O. Douglas who had come to Kentucky to see this unusual valley where bitter controversy had flared. The question was whether or not the Corps should send its contractors into the Red River Gorge with their bulldozers and blasting teams to construct an $11.7 million dam and flood the scenic treasure there.

But the concerned people had come late to rescue

the Red River. Downstream in Clay City, citizens had talked for years of a dam. Some said they had discussed such a project for three decades. There have been floods along the Red River. The people could tick them off on their fingers—'38, '39, '57, '62 they say, and those who would take away their hope of salvation from these wild waters must be heartless and callous. They also admitted the multimillion-dollar influx of federal funds held a basic appeal.

The Sierra Club invited Justice Douglas to lead a hike through the gorge. Newspaper reporters and photographers came. The Louisville *Courier-Journal,* long a powerful and effective force for wise use of natural resources, began a continuing campaign to save the Red River Gorge. Those who hiked the valley that day went home to write letters to their Congressmen.

Such public activity is intensely disliked by the Corps. It much prefers to go about its beaverlike work free of controversy and nasty little time-consuming skirmishes. But increasingly in recent times, its plans have drawn the fire of conservation forces. Such groups, sometimes referred to by Corps leadership as "little old ladies in tennis shoes," make plain their belief that we have already gone too far in permitting the Corps freedom of choice in its selection of new reservoir sites.

The best dam sites have already been identified and used, and the flood plains behind them covered with slack waters. Remaining sites are those of increasingly questionably justification. But, as one Corps worker explained to me in his Washington office, "A dam site is such a rare natural resource, that there should not be all this controversy about using it." Those who disagree insist that too often the rarest natural resources are those covered by water behind the dams.

These were the opposing viewpoints at the heart of the controversy in Kentucky's Red River Gorge.

Kentucky was already richly endowed with great impoundments constructed at federal expense. Fishermen, boaters, and campers for hundreds of miles around are well aware of this. There were already four such lakes within an hour's drive to the south of the Red River location, and one new one planned within an hour's drive to the north. What was planned for the scenic Red River Gorge by the dam builders was no more and no less than one more reservoir.

As for flood control, which was the major benefit claimed for the proposed impoundment, the Corps could have planned the dam for an alternate site 5.8 miles downstream, saving the unique gorge, or considered a flood wall around the Clay City community.

Justice Douglas spoke out sharply against the Corps' plan, citizens continued to write letters, and the Sierra Club and the National Audubon Society campaigned. But in due time, having weighed the opposition, the Corps' determination to build where it first proposed the dam did not change until Kentucky Governor Louie B. Nunn announced that he preferred the lower site. Faced with this added pressure the Corps reluctantly yielded.

The history of the Corps of Engineers begins in the earliest days of the formation of the American Government. There were Army engineers on the scene even before the Revolutionary War, and the present Corps traces its own history back to 1802 when Congress created the Corps and the Military Academy at West Point in the same act. Although most of us are content to use the administrations of the country's presidents as a frame of reference for our national development, the Corps of Engineers, typically, has its own view. It is expressed in its booklet, *Geneses of The Corps of*

Engineers: "Similarly the history of the expansion and development of the nation from the Atlantic States to the Pacific Ocean," says the Corps, "may well be marked by the successive administration periods of our Chief of Engineers."

Congress first introduced the youthful Corps to its civil works responsibilities in 1824. That year the Engineers were allotted $75,000 and directed to remove from the Ohio and Mississippi rivers, "snags, sawyers, planters and other impediment of that nature." Neither Congress nor the Corps could have foreseen how the infant civil works program would flourish.

From that modest beginning the program expanded until today the Corps is the world's largest construction organization, and biggest developer of water control structures. In May, 1967, according to a report from the Office of the Chief of Engineers, the Corps was custodian of 3828 active civil works projects with ". . . a total estimated cost of $30 billion." Of this total, 312 projects were then under construction. The Corps had spent $20.9 billion completing those already finished and maintaining them. Each year the Corps gets about $1.25 billion for its civil works projects.

By 1967 the Corps had refined 19,000 miles of rivers and waterways with dams, reservoirs, levees, deeper channels and other alterations. In the name of flood control it had built more than eight hundred projects, many of which had other benefits claimed for them. Its generating plants at forty-five projects had a 9.5 million kilowatt capacity, about 20 per cent of the nation's total hydroelectric capacity, with another twenty-six projects under construction.

Major Corps projects traditionally begin with agreement between local people, congressional representatives, and Corps personnel concerning the desirability of the plan. Before the Corps begins detailed planning, it must have the authorization of Congress. But the Corps has standing authority to proceed with certain categories of expenditures without bothering the lawmakers. If he thinks small flood-control measures are needed, the Chief of Engineers may authorize them, providing they cost less than $1 million and won't call for added expenditures to solve the problem. The Corps also enjoys a standing authorization to spend up to $50,000 in a location within a single year for streambank protection and up to $100,000 a year on clearing and straightening a stream channel.

Through it all, the Corps maintains its impeccable reputation, free of any hint of scandal in the handling of billions of dollars, a dedicated public servant pursuing its mission as it sees its mission. And there is no denying even by critics, that the Corps has created a long list of credits. Its good works include in addition to flood-control structures, and reservoirs, the completion of the Panama Canal. Where it gets into trouble is in the fact that it has grown steadily and must be constantly tackling more jobs to stay in its position of power and to meet the insatiable demands of Congressmen. They need the Corps to build their pork barrel projects, and the Corps needs Congress to keep it in business.

The Corps, although a branch of the Defense Department, draws its life blood from Congress. The symbiotic relationship betwen Congress and the Corps is of long duration. Congress has jealously guarded its close tie with the Corps. When President Harding once suggested placing the civil works projects in the Department of the Interior, a Joint Committee of Congress quickly rejected the move. In 1932 President Hoover signed an executive order transferring the civil works of the Corps of Engineers to the Department of the Interior in an effort to co-ordinate water-resources works and cut expenditures. Congress nullified the executive order and restored the pampered Engineers to a more independent position.

One civil servant employed by the Corps of Engineers explained to a U. S. Fish and Wildlife Service biologist, "You guys are country boys when it comes to handling Congressmen. We maintain dossiers on each member of appropriations committees. When one of these congressmen came to New Orleans recently for the first time, we were ready for him. One of our people took a friend of his to dinner in Washington just to learn more about him. We found out that he was a diabetic. So when he arrived in New Orleans, his air-conditioned limousine was already equipped with a refrigerator stocked with everything he might need, including insulin."

Superficially, it might appear that the Corps has a built-in safeguard against wasteful projects in its seven-man Rivers and Harbors Board. This group, along with its squadrons of specialists, must pass judgment on the feasibility and economic justification of all major proposals. If a majority of the seven-man board votes "not convinced," the project may be stymied. Then again, it might not be. The Chief of Engineers is in a position to veto the finding of this board of specialists. The Chief of Engineers can pass the finding along with a contrary opinion. The Secretary of the Army can also veto the board's finding, as can the Secretary of Defense or the President of the United States. Congress, in its wisdom, can do the same thing in effect. It is not committed to the finding of the Board of Rivers and Harbors, and if the Board's decision against a project goes on to Congress with a contrary opinion attached by the Chief of Engineers, Congress can accept the contrary opinion as easily as not.

When Senator Robert S. Kerr was stumping for construction of the Arkansas River Basin Project, the Board of Rivers and Harbors studied the prospect with its usual detailed procedure and ruled that it would be uneconomic. It voted against it. But Chief of Engineers Eugene Reybold attached his opinion that the project deserved authorization. Congress, prodded by Senator Kerr, chose to go along with the Reybold opinion. Consequently, the Arkansas River Basin Project, designed to create harbors in the prairies of Oklahoma, has been in the works ever since.

The construction of Corps projects is farmed out to contractors, usually on the basis of competitive bids, and at any one time there are several thousand such contracts underway. Within the Corps, the work is done by 40,000 civil employees supervised by about two hundred regular Army Officers, a military elite historically drawn from the top of West Point's classes. These are the bright young men of the military and in the years ahead each will be exposed to a wide range of schooling.

Such an officer is steeped in the proud tradition of the Corps. He is aware of its spectacular works and dedicated to its mission. His colleagues are highly skilled professionals. The high morale within the Corps extends to its civil force as well. The outsider gains the impression, from civil servant and professional soldier alike, that the Corps can do no wrong and, except for tight budgets, could accomplish much more good. Its works are largely viewed as bargains for the country at large.

Anyone who feels that the Corps must be running out of dam sites and jobs, does an injustice to the exploratory nature of the organization and the imaginative minds of those who compose its forces. I asked one thirty-year civilian employee of the Corps when they were going to run out of valleys to dam. Smilingly, he told me, ". . . there are a lot of valleys." He doubted that they would ever run out of places to build dams. This line of thought inevitably leads to building impoundments in less and less justifiable locations.

Admittedly, there has been some evidence in recent times of a broadening outlook on the part of some Corps workers, a creeping awareness that there may be more to consider in the planning of a grand new dam than the pouring of concrete. In an attempt to adjust its thinking to an evolving public and government attitude, the Corps has added biologists and ecologists to its field staff. In this band of technically trained scientists, the Corps has its own advisers instead of relying completely on scientists in other governmental agencies such as the Department of the Interior, or the Department of Health, Education, and Welfare.

From its early and simple responsibilities dealing with navigation, and then flood control, the Corps has broadened its fields of interests, with congressional authority, to include a wide range of subjects justifying its work. The Corps, with eight million acres of federal land and 28,000 miles of waterways, is also one of the federal government's largest recreation agencies.

The everlasting search for new jobs sometimes brings the Corps to strange and challenging tasks. For many years there has been a compulsion to tidy up Niagara Falls. It is true that rocks have fallen to the bed of the river at the foot of the American Falls. Nature is letting the Falls come apart, as if man were not here to worry about it. But to the Corps of Engineers, Nature, like a fractious child, is to be corrected and improved at every turn. If the rocks of Niagara Falls are out of place, rearrange them. If America is going to have a famous waterfall, let it be a neat, orderly attraction.

How can the Corps rescue the aging Niagara Falls?

Honeymooners relax. We are assured it can be done. Tons of rocks must be moved, and others strengthened. It may never be as neat as Bonneville Dam, but Bonneville has the advantage of having been engineered properly from the beginning.

Added reservoir capacity is often justified as essential water-quality control, or pollution dilution. While visiting one longtime civil employee of the Corps in his Washington office, I noted that this seemed a sad reflection on our civilization. We now must build great costly reservoirs simply to dilute our wastes. Would it not be better to treat the pollution at the source and keep the streams clean than to dilute the sewage?

"Where you have people," he insisted, taking immediate exception to my line of reasoning, "you are going to have wastes. It's as simple as that. Now, Secretary Udall has said that we will not have any further degradation of any streams. I'm not sure this is possible, and I'm not even certain such a policy is wise. How can you have progress without increasing wastes? And the rivers," he added in summary, "are Nature's waste-disposal system."

There arose before me a picture of America seen through these eyes. People are everywhere. Cities reach on and on. Expediency justifies every assault on natural resources, and the nation's streams are a vast sewer system with Corps-constructed reservoirs doing water-closet duty. And always the reservoirs must be giant structures, because the Corps thinks big.

2. Think Big Water

One guiding urgency and dominant interest drives the Corps of Engineers: it thinks big water. It is the big job, the spectacular structure, the multimillion-dollar project, that provides a real challenge. And having evolved to fill the planner's role, the Corps can be expected to see regional planning as a need for big-water structures. It is altogether natural for builders to seek projects to build. The Corps can be expected, by its nature and background, to plan in terms of big projects and to equate wise land use with transforming natural locations into big reservoirs. With such a basic driving philosophy, all other elements in its planning, including wildlife, recreation, and even flood control must bend to fit the big dam concept.

At one time the Corps seemed at odds with other water-management agencies of the federal government, especially the Bureau of Reclamation. The major function of the Bureau of Reclamation is the creation of reservoirs and other water management structures to convert western deserts into productive land. The conflicting interests of the Corps of Engineers and the Bureau of Reclamation came into sharp focus along the Missouri River during the early 1940s. Both government agencies were determined to develop the gigantic river basin, each according to its own responsibility. The struggle began in May, 1943, when Congress passed a resolution calling upon the Engineers to survey the river to see what might be suggested there by way of flood control, irrigation, hydroelectric-power production and irrigation. The Corps assigned Colonel Lewis A. Pick to complete the assignment for Congress.

In the offices of the Bureau of Reclamation, however, this resolution, especially that portion of it speaking of irrigation, aroused definite defense postures, based on well-developed territorial instincts. As traditional builders of irrigation and electric power-producing dams through the west, Reclamation was ready to defend its place in the government pecking order against the Engineers. As for the farmers who would use the water for irrigation, the thought of having the Corps come into the valley was not entirely unwelcome. Bureau of Reclamation projects call for setting up a plan for water users to repay costs of installation on irrigation systems; there was no such provision for the work of the Corps. The water from a Corps reservoir would be free.

One year after Congress turned the Corps loose upon the Missouri, Reclamation came along with its own plan which had been under preparation several years before the Corps was set in motion. It was written by W. Glenn Sloan of the Bureau's office in Billings, Montana. When the resulting disagreement came to President Roosevelt's office, he directed the two agencies to get together on their planning. The resulting Pick-Sloan Plan combined the talents of the Corps dam builders with the responsibilities of the Bureau of Reclamation.

Such controversies seem to have been resolved long since. Today, three building agencies, the Corps of Engineers, the Bureau of Reclamation, and the Soil Conservation Service, have divided the major water-development responsibilities, with all apparently working in harmony and at full speed, each in pursuit of improving its own segment of the landscape. The Soil Conservation Service comes into the picture in the headwaters. It builds ponds and small reservoirs. It also straightens creeks, which would often be better off if left to follow their original paths. Far up in the headwaters SCS co-ordinates its impoundments with the more spectacular downstream structures of the Corps which is scarcely interested, at any rate, in wasting its time and skills on one hundred-acre ponds. The Bureau of Reclamation, like the Corps, favors big projects. These two big-water agencies tend to divide the western landscape geographically, or to combine forces and divide the major watersheds. They have divided Texas, in the Texas Water Plan, generally along the 100th meridian.

Any Corps project big enough to require congressional authorization follows an established pattern in its growth from idea to completed structure. There are, as one Corps publication explains it, eighteen steps in the process. Invariably such a project, the Corps insists, has its beginning with local interest by an aroused or perceptive public seeking the solution to some pressing problem. Theoretically, as people clean up the mud after a devastating flood and count their economic losses they say, "Something must be done." At this point they are well advised to turn to their senator or representative.

Although there are, doubtless, instances where the first thought of such a project does begin with the natives of a valley, there must likewise be times when the cheerleading is set in motion by outside forces. It is unlikely that the the Corps of Engineers, having discovered a fine location for a new reservoir, would sit quietly hoping that local people might call for a lake in that precise location. Such an idea can be planted, perhaps during a speaking engagement at which a Corps public relations man appears at a local fraternal or businessmen's club luncheon, or perhaps during conversation with a member of Congress alert to new possibilities for bringing federal gifts to his constituents.

Whatever the seed from which the project sprouts, the next step is up to the area's representative or senator in Washington. If the project is one that has been previously considered and laid aside for some reason, it can be exhumed for re-examination, as authorized by the Rivers and Harbors Act of 1914. With the passage of time a fresh look sometimes lends new promise to former duds. But if there has never been a report made on the proposed project, the senator or representative can ask the Public Works Committee to include authorization for such a survey in the next Rivers and Harbors Bill. Or he may initiate action in a separate bill.

Then it is up to the committee to which the bill is referred. If this group decides that the proposed dam across Dry Run may indeed transform Nowheresville into a flourishing community, it passes a resolution calling upon the Secretary of the Army to have the Corps of Engineers make the survey. Now, with money available from Congress for the initial investigation, the Chief of Engineers assigns the project to a Division Engineer. He then usually sends it on down to his appropriate district engineers, and the wheels are in full motion.

Now people in the community to be affected are likely to have an opportunity to express their feelings on the proposal. The division or district engineer must set dates for public hearings. Sometimes these gatherings can line up two opposing schools of thought within a community and the evening's event erupts into a heated discussion.

Late in May, 1968, the Huntington, West Virginia, office of the Corps conducted what was perhaps a typical hearing in the assembly hall of a school building in Georgetown, Ohio. Georgetown, the county seat of Brown County, is forty miles east of Cincinnati in the southwestern corner of the state. It is also in the western edge of the Appalachian region, which was important to this hearing. The question was whether or not the Corps should proceed with its plan to construct an impoundment on White Oak Creek, a shallow creek which collects water from the hills of Brown County as it flows south over rocky beds to enter the Ohio River.

Although I had waded White Oak Creek's quiet, secluded pools in pursuit of vigorous smallmouth bass for many years, I harbored no deep-seated prejudice against damming the valley on that score. To me it is not a valley that can be classified as unique among natural wonders. If we must dam a certain percentage of our small valleys, the valley of White Oak seems as logical a choice as the next one. But since it appears that the plans might ultimately call for damming that one too, and also the one next to it, I appeared at the hearing to savor the logic of those stumping for this latest of the proposed impoundments in southwestern Ohio.

Perhaps I would have been less interested except for what had occurred in the next county the year before. Down through Clermont County in which I lived for many years, there flows a forest-fringed stream known as the East Fork of the Little Miami. The East Fork is the last really clean stream within easy-driving distance of the Greater Cincinnati area. It should not have come as any surprise that the Corps was proceeding with plans to construct in the heart of the East Fork, a dam which, at a cost of $25 million, would effectively smother miles of that wild little valley. I attended a hearing on that project in its early days.

That hearing was held in the Batavia High School, and from the first it was obvious that local com-

mercial interests and those hungry for the personal
gains promised by the big influx of federal dollars,
were in solid control. If a vote had been taken on
that day at the Batavia school, the scattered doubters
would have been drowned out by a shout of yea
votes. Most envisioned new riches on the local landscape because of the dam. The fact that they would
in turn sacrifice their rare natural stream seemed of
little concern. The $25 million job looked to Clermont
County like the closest thing to a gold strike since
Sutter dug his millstream. Citizens seemed unable
to relate the cost of the dam to their own tax bills,
or think to ask whether their valley might profit more
in the long run by retaining its natural beauty and
character. The attitude was predictable to the Corps.
They see it at hearing after hearing.

The evening, in 1968, in the Georgetown school
was the same with only slight variations. The colonel
from Huntington was the only one in uniform. There
were tape recorders in operation to catch every word
of testimony, and speakers were asked to talk into
one of the three microphones. The corps prefers that
those offering statements at one of its hearings submit
them in writing, in quadruplicate. Ordinarily, they
are able to assemble an impressive sheaf of supporting evidence in this manner. In advance they send
out notice of the hearing to "interested parties."

At this early hearing there was at least one major
element of information still unavailable to those present. No one was eager to speculate on the eventual
cost of the dam proposed for White Oak Creek. This
would come later. If the hearings went well and the
Corps was assigned to proceed with its latest study
of the project, it would then be expected to compute
a benefit-cost ratio.

This is precisely what it sounds like, a mathematical
expression of the relation of estimated costs to esti-

mated benefits, usually over a period of half a century. To the Corps the benefit-cost ratio can be all-important. If the calculations come out showing cost greater than the dollar benefits promised, the project will not get off the ground. But the fact that the Corps, applying the rules established by Congress, calculates its own b/c ratio enables it to gather a rough idea of whether a project can qualify for building under the rules of the moment, even before going to the trouble of conducting the first public hearings. In the Georgetown meeting, Colonel William D. Falck did speculate that the cost figure might go around $30 million. "But we must think it has some chance of qualifying," he added, "or we wouldn't be here tonight."

That it might qualify with a figure this high is surprising. It had been rejected several years earlier as uneconomical at a cost of about $19 million. After having failed to muster sufficient benefits to hurdle the cost barrier, the White Oak plan was now back— five years later—looking better in spite of a cost increase of nearly 50 per cent. The reasons behind this development should tell the Corps anew what it has already learned from experience: never give up on a proposed big-water project simply because it seems uneconomical at the moment. If circumstances or force of adverse public opinion should compel the Corps planners to withdraw from a budding project, the plan can be salted down for later exhumation. Someday the climate will be more friendly. Many are the projects that have aged for a quarter of a century or more, while the Corps busied itself and its contractors with other matters.

What had resurrected the White Oak Project after its years in limbo was the Appalachian Regional Development Act of 1965. Section 206 of the Act brought the Corps into Appalachian planning in a major role. "The Secretary of the Army," said the Act, "is hereby authorized and directed to prepare a comprehensive plan for the development and efficient utilization of the water and related resources of the Appalachian Region, . . . which plans shall constitute an integral and harmonious component of the regional economic-development program authorized by this act."

Charged with this responsibility in the new program to help bring better times to the depressed communities of Appalachia, the Corps responded by establishing an Office of Appalachian Studies under Colonel J. C. H. Lee in Cincinnati. Colonel Lee and his staff began searching Appalachia for Corps projects that might fit the concept of the new Act.

Time was short. The Administration wanted to get the Appalachian program started. The Corps met this need in two ways. It was not surprising, for example, that the dam builders should at once view big dams as the salvation of Appalachia. Consequently, those assembled in the schoolhouse in Georgetown heard the Engineers explain that their community was lagging behind the rest of the state and the nation in income largely because it did not have the industry it needed, or the population. The reason was to be found in inadequate water supplies. The key then, obviously, was a better source of water. With a lake to supply Georgetown with its long-time water needs, the Corps foresaw that new riches would be forthcoming. In keeping with the concept of the Appalachian program, other agencies, state and federal, had contributed their own segments to the over-all plan. Included would be a wildlife area, a number of smaller upland reservoirs to be built by the Soil Conservation Service, and various recreation areas. Although it was a more comprehensive land-use plan than the Corps usually submits to the people, its big interest was still the reservoir. And no alternative plan involving lower-cost smaller reservoirs was offered.

The Corps Office of Appalachian Studies, I was told by a Corps civil servant, surveyed twelve Corps districts seeking potential projects that fit the Appalachian Act concept. They found them in proposals such as White Oak which had previously failed to measure up. Now, with an element of public work and regional development figured into the benefit side of the ratio, they should display a more favorable benefit-cost ratio. The Corps soon came up with a list of about sixty such projects, eventually narrowed down to seventeen. Some included several impoundments within a single project.

One, long a dream with the Corps, was for a gigantic dam in the steep, wooded mountains of southern Kentucky. If you were to leave the Ohio River, east of Paducah, Kentucky, to journey up its tributary through the valley of the famed Cumberland River, you would travel in both Kentucky and Tennessee. You would go through Nashville, travel eastward, and swing north into Kentucky's hill country to arrive eventually at Wolf Creek Dam behind which are the deep waters of Lake Cumberland. This big inland lake winds back into a thousand hollows. At maximum level its waters back up for 101 miles, and cover 63,530 acres. By the time it was completed in 1950, Lake Cumberland had cost more than $79 million, and scarcely anyone had objected to it.

Near Burnside, Kentucky, is one of the river's major tributaries, the Big South Fork of the Cumberland River. Drive up the Big South Fork where the steep rocky gorges bring new scenic discoveries. When you reach a point known as Devil's Jump, some forty-eight miles above the stream's mouth, stop and take a look around. You have just arrived at one more scenic treasure which the Corps of Engineers has staked out for improvement.

Seeking the authorization for Devil's Jump, the Corps submitted to Congress in May, 1961, its favorable report recommending ". . . improvement of Big South Fork for power production, flood control and other purposes, by construction of a dam at the Devil's Jump site at about river mile 48.1."

For this rocky, scenic valley and its river which has been widely recommended for inclusion in the national Wild Rivers program, the Corps planned a dam 483 feet high, to back water up the valley twenty-nine miles and cover 37,000 acres. The reservoir would also back waters up permanently some sixteen miles into Clear Fork, another scenic gorge with spectacular sandstone walls. Since that time, these streams have grown increasingly popular with wilderness adventurers and especially canoeists. In the years between 1960 and 1965, according to a Bureau of Outdoor Recreation publication, canoeing here increased by 65 per cent. During the summer of 1968 the South Fork was the site of the National Championship Marathon of the U. S. Canoe Association. In its 1964 report urging that this stream be kept wild, the Bureau of Outdoor Recreation estimated that the valley could absorb half a million visitor-days annually and still retain its wonderfully wild character. Conservationists pointed out that such wild rivers were at a definite premium, especially in the Kentucky and Tennessee area where numerous man-made reservoirs already exist.

And the Corps had run into early trouble in its effort to put Devil's Jump into the "authorized" category. It simply did not look like a paying proposition. Independent engineering studies demonstrated that the costs of current generated at Devil's Jump would run eight to ten times as high as the cost of power produced by TVA, the agency the Corps anticipated would be marketing the power. Understandably, TVA did not want to buy this uneconomical power. As late as April 29, 1968 an official of TVA said that the cost of this power would be ". . . too high to be usable in our system."

Likewise, flood-control benefits of the proposed Devil's Jump dam had not shown great promise. The fact was that Wolf Creek Dam downstream was doing what needed to be done on flood control. Unfortunately, from the Corps point of view, unless such a reservoir could promise some flood-control benefits, Congress in those years was not interested. This impasse led the Corps to one of its more clever plans.

Its solution was simply not to drain Lake Cumberland down as low as usual for the winter. Automatically, this would mean that Lake Cumberland no longer had storage capacity to hold back as much water during periods of high run-off. Then these waters, for which there had been no room left in Lake Cumberland, could be accommodated in the proposed Devil's Jump Reservoir. This, at least in theory, would enable the Corps to claim that Devil's Jump would hold back 256,000 acre-feet of water for flood control in spite of the fact that it offered no such benefits in any real sense. In an announcement of an approaching hearing scheduled for May 9, 1968, Colonel Jesse L. Fishback of the Nashville District, said, "This in effect constitutes a transfer of reservoir capacity which, while entailing no change in flood-control efficiency, would result in a net gain in power potential on a system basis through increased power production at Wolf Creek and other hydroelectric plants downstream." He failed to note that the added power would arrive at the market considerably after TVA had swung heavily into the more economical atomic type power-generating plants.

So, with its flood-control features obviously phony, and its power production unpromising, what else could the Corps hold up before Congress to entice it into committing the country to an expenditure of an estimated $151 million for Devil's Jump? It had a few lesser cards in its hand. There was the usual "wildlife enhancement." Of this, Liane B. Russell, President of the Tennessee Citizens for Wilderness Planning, said as a witness before the Corps' hearing, "It is difficult to see how wildlife would be enhanced by innundating 37,000 acres of its natural habitat." Primarily this left recreation, and here again the Corps was having a difficult time because of the abundance of big lakes nearby, including Lake Cumberland, and because the banks of Devil's Jump promised to be mudflats during those months when the reservoir was drawn down.

Congress, to its credit, had formerly refused to go along with the Corps on Devil's Jump. Consequently, by 1965 the Corps saw the new approach to the problems of Appalachia as the salvation of Devil's Jump. It became a Corps answer to the government search for ways to funnel new wealth into Appalachia.

On May 9, 1968, the Corps conducted still another hearing on Devil's Jump at Whitley City, Kentucky, where those favoring the expenditure steam-rollered the handful of opponents speaking in favor of retaining the stream in its free-flowing nature. In one prepared statement after the other, local organizations responded to the Corps' plea and spoke of their unqualified support for a dam at Devil's Jump. The district representative to Congress sent a letter supporting the project. The deck was well stacked and those who spoke for moderation and preservation of the natural beauty of the valley were jeered by some of their neighbors. There was testimony that this was a depressed region and there seemed to be widespread feeling that the influx of $151 million would be a Godsend. In such an atmosphere there is little consideration given to abuse of the natural landscape.

The 90th Congress revived some hope of saving the Big South Fork by lifting out of the Omnibus Rivers and Harbors Flood Control Bill an item that would have authorized the dam at Devil's Jump. The Act did not stop there, however, but called upon the Chief of Engineers, the Secretary of Agriculture, and the Secretary of the Interior to submit to Congress a committee report which it would use to help solve the sticky and much-debated question of whether to dam the Big South Fork or designate it a wild river. Such a wild river designation would cost the Corps a valley site which it considers a natural for its special talents.

But there is more at stake than big dams and temporary welfare. The creation of reservoirs permanently removes acreage from any other use. Is the sacrifice of one more valley the best possible course of action in a land being increasingly flooded beneath big reservoirs? Is big water really better in the White Oak Valley—and a thousand more—than a system of smaller reservoirs upstream? The objective answer is hardly to be found within the Army Corps of Engineers.

Basic among the questions involved is whether it is wise to permit the Engineers to assume the role of the regional planner. With their tendency to think big there will be no end to water-control challenges. Where a river silts up—dredge it. When it runs crooked—straighten it. Where it runs straight—deepen it. Where it runs at all—stop it. And where it doesn't run—build a canal.

3. Sweet and Sour Pork

If you should ever feel the urge to serve your neighbors in the halls of Congress, one of the earliest lessons you must learn is not to trip over the pork barrel. One youthful southern Ohio attorney made this mistake in the mid-1960s only to end up bruised and disillusioned.

His opponent, the incumbent, had spent a large portion of his time in Washington stumping for a multimillion-dollar Corps of Engineer busy-work project to dam what was the only clean, free-running little river remaining in southwestern Ohio, a stream noted for its wooded valley and wild beauty.

The neophyte politician was taken in tow by a crusading weekly newspaper editor who drove him out to the condemned valley. He showed him where the dam would be, and explained how the millions of dollars sought for damming this stream might better be used almost anywhere else.

The hopeful candidate sensing a genuine campaign issue, a real waste of public funds, grew excited, and rushed off to Washington to tell his party leaders what he had uncovered. He proposed to shake up the opposition. Expecting his party leaders to join in his exuberance, he was shaken by their stony-faced reaction. They looked silently from one to the other. "I thought," said the innocent beginner, "they were shocked at this flagrant waste of tax money. Then I began to realize they were astounded by my naïveté instead."

On that day he learned one of the basic facts of Washington political life—don't rock the boat that's carrying the pork barrel. He was pointedly told to lay off the anti-dam issue or, "Don't expect any help from this office." As it turned out his principles were never tested; the incumbent, promising millions of dollars to his constituents via the multimillion-dollar dam project, won handily.

What the budding politician had failed to comprehend was the protective attitude of Congress over its pork barrel domain, a consistently strong element in political careers all over the country. At the same time, for example, in the beautiful, wild country of northern Maine there was a pork barrel skirmish that created such controversy that years will not heal the scars.

This massive construction project, known as "Dickey-Lincoln," was conceived primarily as a multimillion-dollar consolation prize. The story had its beginning in the spectacular tides of the Bay of Fundy which twice a day come surging inland, raising the water levels in the bay more than forty feet. What comes in, must go out, and the amount of water in each of these giant tides has been computed at more than 3600 billion cubic feet.

That this source of potential power might be tapped for the generation of electricity is an idea that goes back at least half a century. Over the years the possibility came up for congressional consideration. But eventually it was dismissed because of a combination of high cost and the fact that the coming and going of the tides was not co-ordinated with peak power.

Next, attention turned to the more common practice of simply damming one more old-fashioned river, and constructing there an orthodox power plant so that taxpaying New Englanders might be endowed with their share of pork from the bottomless barrel.

Where could the Engineers build a dam in the Maine countryside? There was the St. John River some two hundred miles to the North and the proper place on it, said the Corps of Engineers, seemed to be in the vicinity of two small towns—Lincoln School and Dickey. Congress, and just about everyone else, was to hear more about Dickey-Lincoln in the months ahead than they really cared to hear, as Maine's two senators and assorted representatives lined up in support of the project and worked long and hard in its behalf.

They obtained enough congressional support in 1965 to gain Senate authorization. The best way to gain approval in the House of Representatives was the common practice of imbedding the issue in an omnibus Rivers and Harbors Bill. But for Dickey-Lincoln there were storms ahead. Even with the cherished authorization secured, there was trouble convincing Congress it should allocate funds for planning the project.

As might be expected, New England power companies lined up early in determined, solid opposition to Dickey-Lincoln and its threat of government-produced kilowatts. But more was involved than a struggle between private and public power.

Conservationists and economists both offered arguments that could not be lightly dismissed. The Corps of Engineers had duly computed the price of the Dickey-Lincoln job, including the transmission lines to carry the power 340 miles south to the Boston area where there seemed some chance of marketing it. The estimated cost was $380 million. But this was figured at 1966 levels with no added computations to take into account the steadily rising costs of construction during the years it was in the works. Private power, meanwhile, claimed it could build facilities to supply the same amount of power at a cost of $75 million, and, not surprisingly, contended that there was no real need for the added power.

The political leaders, and others favoring the project, said the opposition was the product of massive lobbying by private power companies. The charges and countercharges only served to fog the issue.

But there was another aspect which, through the coming decades, might be even more significant to the Northeast than the cost of the kilowatt. This was the question of whether or not to flood out 100,000 acres of magnificent Maine wild country. In October, 1967, the Maine State Biologists Association added its voice. The association's president, Dr. Robert M. Chute of the Department of Biology, at Bates College in Lewiston, explained that the biologists were not so much interested in the question of public versus private power as they were in the lack of good planning for Maine's future development. Stating that the proposed project might have made sense as a public works program in the 1930s, they believed that a more economical solution today would be atomic-power plants constructed closer to the area where the power would find its market.

Even more important, the biologists felt, was the question of whether to inundate one of the remaining rare areas which holds economic promise as an outdoor-recreation area. The statement called for "Regionalized planned development of our resources to insure the future of both industrial and recreational aspects of our economy. Unplanned pork barrel development," they added, "can weaken both."

Such pronouncements brought the usual accusations that the objecting biologists were serving the cause of private power interests. There were derogatory references in the letter columns of regional weekly newspapers about the "chickadee-loving conservationists." Dr. Chute commented further on why he thought Dickey-Lincoln would be a debasement of the Maine landscape. "The point the conservationists are trying to make," he wrote in a letter to the Portland *Press-Herald*, "is a serious, well-considered one. They believe the best conservation and development use for the Upper St. John region is to preserve a wild river; feeling this has greater recreation and resource value than an artificial lake of dubious quality. Only the shortsighted can fail to see how rapidly the truly wild areas of New England are vanishing." Dr. Chute made it clear that he was, ". . . against Dickey but for public power." Although he said he would not even keep utilities stock ". . . if it were given to me." He added, "Let's not endanger our future in our enthusiasm to fight the private power companies."

Through it all the Corps leaned quietly on its shovel and waited patiently. With the project authorized, a major barrier has been cleared. The authorization carries no expiration date, and the possibility that the Corps will recommend to Congress deauthorization is slim indeed. More probably, as the Corps realizes, Congress will, in its own time, make available the funds for Dickey-Lincoln to smother the St. John Valley. Farewell to one more American river.

If there was one reason the senators and representatives of Maine and nearby New England states felt Dickey-Lincoln should be constructed by the federal government, it was the obvious fact that this area had not had its share of big government construction. Other parts of the country had fared better. Across the west were grand, sprawling reclamation projects totaling millions of dollars in cost. The Corps of Engineers had been dispatched to take care of requests in Florida, Texas, Kentucky, Illinois, Arkansas, and just about every other corner of this grand land. Now it was Maine's turn.

To a disturbingly large degree, this type of thinking has dominated our nationwide water-resources program. It was not created by plan, but by grab bag.

Many of the projects on which the Corps of Engineers works in any given year are included in the annual Rivers and Harbors Bill, informally referred to as "The Pork Barrel." The term is believed to go back to the days of slavery. As a special treat, Old Massa would call his slaves around him, then knock the top off a barrel of preserved pork. There would follow a mad rush with everyone reaching into the barrel for as big a chunk of pork as he could get. History has failed to credit the perceptiveness of the person who first noted the similarity of this custom and the handing out of choice federal projects, following only the rule that he who has the longest reach gets the biggest prize.

But the pork barrel has become a way of political life. Politicians too often believe they can equate their worth to their home districts with the amount of money sent back from the federal treasury. Although there are other cuts of pork, such as post office buildings, the choice ones are the impressive big water projects. The Rivers and Harbors Bill usually contains a hodgepodge of costly water projects scattered from Maine to Hawaii. The individual Congressman has his eye on the project closest to his heart, which is to say, nearest to his voting booth. He might sense that projects within the bill are a waste of federal funds, but he is reluctant to argue against his fellow-Congressman's favorite dam or canal. To do so is to jeopardize the other's support for his own pet project.

Typically, the Rivers and Harbors Act of 1965 authorized fifty-three new projects in twenty-three states. In its annual report for 1965, the Corps totaled expenditures of $1,198,498,520 for civil works. Significantly, the Rivers and Harbors Act frequently amends former Rivers and Harbors acts upward. In 1965 the act amended the 1960 act on several projects. It struck out one $2 million item and inserted, "in lieu thereof

$10,000,000." Another allowance of $200,000 became $500,000, one for $3 million was changed to $10 million, while another project computed to cost $400,000 was increased by 25 per cent.

On several occasions presidents have sought authority to veto portions of the Rivers and Harbors bills and Congress, always jealous of this grab-bag legislation, has consistently denied such authority to the Chief Executive and insisted that he take the whole bill as handed to him.

More often than not, the blame for marginal or wasteful projects rests as much, if not more, on the shoulders of Congress and the business interests they serve, as it does with the Corps of Engineers. Between 1910 and 1968, according to Major Frederick J. Clarke, deputy chief of engineering, the Corps has recommended against construction on 4700 of the studies that Congress has assigned it to make and favorably on 3400. There have been cases where the Engineers were notably unenthusiastic but still were ordered full-speed ahead on some Congressman's favorite pork barrel idea. One such project authorized in 1946 was planned to connect the Tennessee and Tombigbee rivers in Mississippi and Alabama with a navigable channel 253 miles long and with ten locks providing a total lift of 341 feet. The cost, in case some taxpayer should ask, was figured at $316 million.

Figure as it would, the Corps of Engineers could not get greatly worked up over the anticipated benefits from the big waterway. When the calculations were completed, the benefit-cost ratio came out 1.24 to 1. To reach this "profit-making" conclusion, the engineers had tossed in all the benefit ingredients they could justify from among those allowed by Congress, including several million dollars for recreation, fish and wildlife "enhancement," and wage payments to those employed to work on the canal. With these dubious benefits stripped away, the Tennessee-Tombigbee Waterway stood like a naked maiden trying to cover up a benefit-cost ratio of 1.01 to 1—a penny on the dollar over half a century!

The Chief of Engineers sent the report along to the Secretary of the Army with his opinion that the 1.24 to 1 figure made the Tennessee-Tombigbee plan economically justifiable. The Secretary of the Army Stanley Resor disagreed, and to his credit tried to tell the lawmakers as much. His letter to Congress called it only "marginally" justified. It lacked the margin of economic safety, he explained, which should mark federal water-development projects. But greedily awaiting the report were powerful legislators from the states to benefit from the influx of federal funds. The report went sailing through the Appropriations Committee. The Corps of Engineers was ordered to get on with this expenditure of public funds, and the Secretary's adverse opinion was not even taken to the floor of Congress for consideration.

One of the country's early canals was a private job in the Santee-Cooper area of South Carolina. This project, completed in 1800, was eventually followed up by the Corps which completed a canal connecting the Santee and Cooper Rivers in 1942. The canal job which brought lasting fame to the Corps of Engineers, however, was the one across the Isthmus of Panama, made possible by the treaty of 1903. The first ship passed along the fifty-mile ditch on August 15, 1914, thus beginning a new epoch in transportation. For the Engineers it had an incalculable public relations value.

On the west coast, California has its outstanding example in the deep-channel canal the Corps dug between the San Francisco port and Sacramento. This sediment-choked ditch had opposition over the years from a lengthy list of notable opponents including the Bureau of the Budget and the Second Hoover Commission. When first recommended by the Corps of Engineers in 1946, the forty-three-mile-long canal was priced at a modest $10,742,000. Even at that price the benefit-cost ratio came out about even—roughly one dollar returned for each dollar invested. In spite of the Bureau of the Budget's thumbs down verdict, a logrolling Congress approved the canal, and in 1949 appropriated the first funds for its construction. By then the price had gone up to an estimated $16 million. The soaring cost had not stopped yet. Six years later the price was computed to be $35 million, or three times the first price. Strangely, the Corps of Engineers—in spite of the multiplied costs—still proved that benefits would exceed the investment. An independent study by the Stanford Research Institute, however, calculated the benefit-cost ratio at .83 to 1, or a return to the taxpayers of America of $83 on each $100 invested. By June 30, 1966, the 30-foot deep channel had cost $41 million.

Was the Sacramento River Canal essential to the national welfare? Such canals generally have only a localized value—restricted to a few preferred industries. The California scheme lacked even this justification because the harbor at San Francisco already had more facilities for seagoing ships than business justified.

Among river navigation promoters the Ohio River is often exhibit number one. This great navigable stream—America's busiest river—is credited with having brought riches and industry to the entire valley because it was made fit for barge traffic. Usually overlooked, in such arguments, are the combined effects of the networks of railroads, highways, and airlines. The Ohio is a great and valuable resource but to hint that the fertile and wealthy Ohio Valley would be a desert except for its subsidized river barges is obviously absurd.

Occasionally there is a canal suggestion even too ridiculous for the politically powerful to push through. One gigantic ditch that barely missed was the dream of Congressman Michael J. Kirwan, a powerful political force from the Youngstown, Ohio, area. Kirwan's 120-mile canal would link Lake Erie with the Ohio River at a point thirty miles northwest of Pittsburgh.

First envisioned by George Washington, this canal was periodically studied and consistently rejected down the years. In this century the plan has been revived several times, usually at the behest of Youngstown industrialists who stand to gain incalculable profits from such federal gifts. More than once, in cases such as this, where common reason should bury the plan for all time, a powerful politician has managed to keep it alive. Rep. Kirwan knew how to apply the full measure of his powerful position as Chairman of the House Appropriations Subcommittee on Public Works. Consequently, the Lake Erie-Ohio River Canal did not die quietly. When Rep. Kirwan succeeded in having the Corps of Engineers sent back to refigure costs and benefits on his pet project, they did not let him down. The pork barrel prize assumed a cloak of respectability. It would cost more than a billion dollars to construct the canal and the harbors, reservoir, and other works that were part of the plan. But, according to the Corps' latest calculations, the benefits would be more than that—the benefit-cost ratio was established at 1.3 to 1. In March, 1967, General William F. Cassidy, Chief of Engineers, announced that the proposed Lake Erie-Ohio River Canal had his approval. The sugarplum was about to fall into eager hands. But a murmur of dissent arose.

Many Congressmen could plainly see the folly of

this gigantic public waste, but they knew enough to keep quiet. Michael J. Kirwan's subcommittee could snatch away their own favorite pork barrel projects to leave them standing empty-handed before the electorate.

Fortunately there are, scattered through the halls of Congress, some legislators determined to call them straight. One who stepped into the deep waters of the proposed canal was Representative Joseph P. Vigorito of Erie, Pennsylvania, who denounced the plan as a "costly boondoggle," of underestimated costs and overestimated benefits. Meanwhile, the state and local governments in the Ohio and Pennsylvania districts to be affected began to understand that not all of the money for Rep. Kirwan's artificial river was to come out of Washington. The plans called for cities and states to build bridges, buy lands, equip harbors, relocate highways, and chip in funds for public parks and marinas to the tune of many millions of dollars. There are few measures calculated to make local people take a closer look at pork barrel projects than the knowledge that part of the cost must come from local sources. Increasingly, the Ohio canal plan was referred to in print as a "boondoggle." There was a critically definitive article in *Reader's Digest*, which brought it national attention. Mail began to flow into congressional offices asking questions about Mike's ditch. Congress was strongly for ". . . getting Mike his ditch," and approved preliminary expenditures which promised to start the project rolling.

How this was steered through the legislative process is a pointed lesson in pork barrel procedures. Kirwan had seen to it that the same bill included big appropriations for engineering works in many other states. Kirwan reminded his fellow Congressman, as he met them in the halls, that this bill held good things for them too, and that, in addition, his committee had steered hundreds of millions of dollars worth of public works projects through Congress in the past. The time had come to collect on past favors. Both the House and Senate passed the bill, not by roll call, but by voice vote, so the names of those for and against were lost. It looked now as if the ditch was going through.

Then, Governor Raymond P. Shafer of Pennsylvania said his state would not guarantee the portion of the costs which planners had assigned it. This was a serious blow. Ohio's Governor James A. Rhodes, characteristically, got off the hook by claiming the need for more time to study the whole thing. To Governor Shafer, whose stand probably played the significant role in saving the American taxpayer a billion dollars or more, should go some fitting citation of appreciation. Although quiet at the moment, this extravagant idea could surface again someday.

Meanwhile, work proceeds on a giant canal being constructed from the banks of the Mississippi up into the sun-baked heart of the Oklahoma prairies. Known as the Arkansas River Navigation Project, this 516-mile-long canal will always stand as a classic pork barrel monument. It was the crowning achievement of the late Senator Robert S. Kerr. Born to a relatively poor family in Ada, Oklahoma, in 1896, Bob Kerr rose to become governor of his state, then for many years one of the most powerful men in the United States Senate. He seldom made any pretense to hide the fact that he was steadily amassing a multimillion-dollar fortune in oil, uranium, and other resources. Much of his work in the legislative halls was related to industries in which he was personally involved. A champion of the depletion allowances and other special legislative favoritism, Senator Kerr envisioned in the efforts of the Army Corps of Engineers great promise for the financial growth of his section of the country. Reaching up from the Mississippi into the dusty center of his home state, was the Arkansas River, which, in spite of shallowness and a rich load of sediment, looked for all the world to Kerr like the Ruhr or the Ohio. It had only to be blessed with the midas touch of the Corps.

According to Kerr's book, *Land, Wood and Water*, it was the fine performance of the Army Engineers that accounted for the "overwhelming" rejection of periodic efforts to form an Arkansas Valley Authority which, like TVA, might have brought regional planning and broader local control to the area. The people were convinced, claimed Kerr that with the Engineers on the job, the Arkansas was in the right hands.

He told of the 1956 dinner staged in Oklahoma to honor the Chief of Engineers, Major General E. C. Itschner. The general spoke glowingly of what the great canal would do to build industries such as oil and chemicals. This must have been music to Bob Kerr, who held great investments in those days in oil and chemicals.

So silt-laden are the Arkansas and Verdigris rivers along which this canal extends, that silt retention structures alone were budgeted at $133 million by the Engineers. Part of the system will include a system of big lakes to keep water in the canal the year around, and eighteen dams and locks to lift and lower barges as they inch inland toward their inland harbor.

What will it cost us to rearrange the Oklahoma-Arkansas landscape so barges can go from the Mississippi River up to Catoosa in northeastern Oklahoma? Only $1.2 billion, claim the Engineers. But it will exceed that, when all the adding machines are finished with the bills.

Although the construction cost of this prairie waterway is staggering, the costs do not end with the project's completion. Operating costs and the endless task of keeping the nine-foot channel free of the river's offering of sediment promises to make the Arkansas Navigation Project a perpetual federal housekeeping chore of great expense. Noted economist, Cecil B. Haver, after studying the project in detail, and perhaps with greater objectivity than did its government proponents, concluded that once this project was completed, the nation might best be served by abandoning it.

Up through those hot dry lands, this costly waterway passes the holdings of citizens as conservative as any in America. I've heard them at one minute curse the federal government and its wasteful practices, and go on the following minute to praise the foresight of those who conceived and promoted the Arkansas River Navigation Project. Public reaction to such boondoggles bears a direct relationship to proximity. Too often, waste of federal funds becomes justified expenditures in our own backyards.

The possibilities that the Arkansas River Navigation Project will return its cost of more than a billion dollars are minimal. Instead, a small group of powerful people with special interests are the beneficiaries.

After Senator Kerr's death in 1963, others rose to carry on. In 1968 Congressman Wilbur D. Mills was Chairman of the House Ways and Means Committee. The battle cry was economy, and the Corps of Engineers, along with other agencies, had to make cuts in its budget request. It came out of the deliberations with a cut of $83 million in its one and a quarter billion dollar request. But Arkansas, as one statistician in the Corps' Washington office explained to me, had not been cut proportionately with other parts of the country. This was because of the Arkansas River Navigation Project. Much of the work was already contracted, and with its continuing contracts, the Corps finds it difficult to implement fast cutbacks on such works. With $135 million appropriated for the Arkansas projects for 1969, Congressman Wilbur Mills could still smile as he went back to his home community, Kensett, Arkansas (pop. 900).

The waste of $50 million on an uneconomic dam or canal does not automatically justify the waste of another $50 million to complete the project. It might be far wiser for Congress to accept the loss to date on such projects as the Cross-Florida Barge Canal, and the Arkansas Navigation Project, deauthorize them and save the money not yet wasted on them.

The Corps of Engineers says it is only the builder of what Congress tells it to build. But the symbiosis is obvious. Under pressure, Congressmen have been known to blithely hand the blame to the very taxpayer shouldered with paying off the grand debt. "If the American people demand of us that we engage in uneconomic projects," they seem to say, "we have no course but to do their bidding."

The Congressman who insists that he is only doing the taxpayers' bidding by pushing for a new reservoir may be guilty of two transgressions. The project probably did not really gain big public support until there was a show of government interest. Secondly, there is no justification for falling back on the weak and indefensible argument that the voters are to blame. Good legislators are usually supplied with more facts on such matters than are their constituents. So, let them lead. Deny the refuge of this weak argument to those who would tap the public treasury simply to secure their own positions. When men in Congress begin to ask publicly whether or not it is really in the national interest to dam Mud Crick, or dig a canal through the Everglades, we will be a little closer to saner use of America's dwindling natural landscape.

4. Strange Ditch in the Everglades

South of Lake Okeechobee the land slopes so gently that the incline is lost to the human eye. Shallow, unhurried water spreads in broad sheets, flowing through the maze of saw grass toward the south. This is the broadest river in North America, the Everglades, sometimes ninety miles wide. It is a vast, level, grassy region, dotted with tree hammocks, the refuge of bobcat, alligator, white-tailed deer, delicate water birds, and countless minute creatures, each with its own niche in the food chain. In all the world there is no place else like it.

On one visit to this unique area, I drove out of the agricultural center of Homestead, along the smooth Highway 1 toward Key Largo. Men had been busy since my last trip into that enchanted subtropical world. Near the eastern border of Everglades National Park there appeared before me a neat bridge, built of concrete and steel, simple in line, and gleaming white beneath a fresh coat of paint. Beneath it was a new sea-level canal, its banks uniformly sloped and as straight as proud engineers could draw them, one more irrevocable step in the everlasting effort to control the gentle waters that inch southward across the broad Everglades toward the sea.

Away to the north the broad canal made a yellow incision across the grassy wetlands. To the south, the canal rounded a sharp bend then disappeared from sight shortly before emptying into the tidal flats of

Barnes Sound. Neatly lettered on the corner of the bridge, like the label on a test tube, was the designation of this new man-made waterway. This was the famous C-111.

At a wide place in the highway I stopped my car. Traffic whined past me. Birds of the subtropics flashed whites, grays, browns, and blacks against the deep-blue Florida sky. The canal beneath this bridge threatened their world with permanent and damaging changes—except for one fact. Below the bridge and from bank to bank, there was a plug of the original earth still in place. Two lanes wide, it had carried the detoured traffic, while contractors built the bridge. But, more important, it had blocked the salt water from the fresh-water marsh above the highway.

Without that plug of earth, high tides and high winds would have carried the strong salt water a dozen miles or more into the heart of the Everglades National Park. This thumb of the park on its eastern edge has been moistened with fresh water through the eons, and wild creatures living there depend on fresh water. I recalled the words of Alexander Sprunt IV, Research Director for the National Audubon Society. This corner of the big and unique park was, Sprunt had explained, ". . . exceedingly rich in wildlife and very important to several species which are considered rare and endangered.

"Over half of Florida's roseate spoonbills breed within the area. More than half of the reddish egrets and a third of the wood storks of eastern North America breed and feed here," he added. These wetlands were also the nesting grounds for one-fourth of the world's remaining population of the magnificent great white herons that stand three feet high in the tidal marshes. Among their neighbors were a number of breeding pairs of the increasingly rare bald eagles, as well as all the North American population of the endangered American crocodile living deep in the seldom traveled wilderness and bothering no one.

This was the wild region into which the neatly fashioned C-111 would carry salt water, while hurrying the life-giving fresh water out to sea. The disaster would come with removal of the yellow plug of earth below the bridge, and the Army Corps of Engineers and the Central and South Florida Flood Control District were eager to complete the canal. As the bridge was finished in 1966, the contractor was standing by with his dragline awaiting word to pull the plug. A single telephone call would give the order.

Meanwhile, a storm of public opinion had risen in defense of the Everglades. The Engineers had made no provision for any structure to block salt water from entering Everglades National Park, which lies at the lower end of the "river of grass."

Where the Everglades have been drained to the south of Okeechobee, lay the muck lands, a thick mantle of spongy, fertile organic soils. Developers had seen the promise in them. Dry out these lands so they could be farmed, they said. But control the water so crops could be irrigated. From these "wastelands" would come food for human consumption, and to those producing it, wealth.

Draining the standing water from the rich soils of the Everglades was no bright new idea by this time. It had been tried as early as 1881 when the state set about a drainage scheme. There followed an age of overoptimistic speculation, and on its heels in 1925, the grand collapse of the whole project. Then came devastating hurricanes, followed in 1929 by the arrival of the Great Depression. Gone for then was the once flowering hope that the agricultural production of these drained black soils would pay off their bonded indebtedness. Twenty million dollars was still needed to complete the planned canals, levees, channels and floodgates.

In 1941, the Reconstruction Finance Corporation bought the refinanced bonds, but still the plan wobbled along. In a 1950 report of the President's Water Resources Commission we find that "Drainage was instituted without knowledge of the amount of water to be handled, the levels to be maintained, or the effect of drainage on the soil. As a result no canals were of the proper size or shape to meet demands, the drainage effort was unsuccessful, and many farming ventures were lost."

Any fault in these failures were not, we should hurry to explain, attributable to the U. S. Army Corps of Engineers. They were not in the Everglades until Congress dispatched them to the scene in 1948 for flood control work. The expert Engineers took over where others had failed and did, one must admit, succeed in reducing the Everglades to a condition of servitude.

Although Florida's developers had no compunction about accepting federal funds and the aid of the Corps, they wanted control of the situation to rest firmly in local hands. To accomplish this, the state organized, in 1949, the Flood Control District which takes over operation of structures which the Corps creates. The Flood Control District and the state contribute some funds, but about 82 per cent of the construction cost of south Florida water projects has come from the federal treasury at the rate of $12 to $14 million a year in recent times. The project will cost at least an estimated $396 million when completed.

At the very tip of Florida, fringed in mangroves, and touched by the salt water of the Florida Bay is the Everglades National Park, depending for its water on its age-old source the overflow waters from Okee-chobee and the conservation areas to the north.

Established in 1947, the Everglades National Park spreads across 1,306,509 acres, one-seventh of the Everglades. It is the only park of its kind. It stands in contrast to the great mountainous national parks of the Rockies, the deserts of the Southwest or the heavily timbered slopes of the Great Smoky Mountains. People come, a million and more a year, to Everglades National Park to see this world of palm trees, grass, and alligators, and to watch the rare birds that walk on stilts. It is a wild, fragile, and beautiful corner of America. In the long range, the welfare of south Florida can only benefit from preserving these magnificent wild lands.

In public addresses before the Florida State Convention of the Izaak Walton League in Miami, in May, 1966, Roger W. Allin, Superintendent of the National Park, gave conservationists his ideas of the importance of that majestic wet ecosystem. "These waters are nursery grounds," he said, "for the men-haden which supports by far the greatest fishery of the United States, the black mullet . . . the spotted sea trout, snook, tarpon, red drum, mangrove snapper, pompano, and, of course, the valuable pink shrimp. Most of these species spawn offshore, but the young and juvenile stages soon move into the estuarine waters to feed and escape predation. Of course the adult of the pompano and the trout remain in the estuarine environments into adulthood. Continued flow of fresh water into and through the park, thence into the estuarine environment is essential to maintain the proper ecological balances . . . Let me make perfectly clear to you that the world-famous sport fisheries of Florida Bay are in a large part dependent on the quantities and quality of fresh water which flows through Everglades National Park."

In addition to these park officials concerned about C-111, there were farm interests to the north whose lands might also be drenched with the killing salt water, once the canal was opened. As the day approached, a rising tide of objections confronted the Engineers. The National Park Service had urged all along that its planners construct in C-111 a salt-water control device to make the ditch safe for the Everglades. This plea had been systematically brushed aside. If the Engineers said such a safeguard was not needed, then according to the Engineers it clearly was not needed.

Originally the purpose of this canal had been to carry excess waters from the farmlands, out to sea. But before the Engineers could finish it, a new element entered the land management picture in that corner of south Florida. In the early 1960s, Florida politicians in general, and those of Dade County in particular, were overjoyed with the prospect of gigantic industrial growth, a promised benefit of the space program. Moving into the wetlands just east of Everglades National Park was the giant Aerojet General, which would use this location for the manufacture of solid fuel for space ships. The company purchased 50,000 acres at bargain rates offered by a grateful state government, and obtained options on another 25,000 acres. The price of Everglades land in that area skyrocketed. The new plant, so the reports predicted, would employ up to 13,000 workmen.

The giant rocket motors would be shipped down by barge from Philadelphia, and that posed a problem. How would they be moved inland to the Aerojet plant? It would be simple enough if Canal-111, the Corps of Engineers' drainage ditch, could be enlarged enough to handle heavy barge traffic. So the fourteen-mile canal became a navigation channel twelve feet deep. The fixed bridge, which was to cost $154,000, was replaced in the plans with a drawbridge at a price of $730,000, part of it charged to Aerojet, the remainder to the Flood Control District, the Florida State Road Department, and the U. S. Treasury.

Eventually the Corps announced that the plug would come out on March 20, 1967. Then, if all those concerned amateurs were right, and wind and tide did indeed damage the park and the farmlands to the north with salt water, the Engineers would consider installing a structure to correct the situation. The Flood Control District claimed this was the way to learn who was right. The National Park Service was not so much interested in proving its point as in saving the park.

Actually, there was nothing to keep the Engineers from pulling the plug. There was no final authority above them, and nothing the Park Service could do. Day by day, they waited for the inevitable, expecting at any time to learn that the dragline had clawed away the block of earth.

But, meanwhile, the word spread and people across the country were making it known that the fate of the Everglades National Park was, after all, important to citizens everywhere. "There are sadly, but perhaps not so strangely," said the National Audubon Society's Charles H. Callison, "some powerful groups which resent the National Park because it stands in the way of covetous ambitions to turn every square mile of Florida into cropland, real estate developments, or industrial sites."

Finally, with only five days left, the National Audubon Society, using a legal tool new to it, went into a federal court to seek an injunction against the U. S. Army Corps of Engineers to prevent them from opening the canal without first installing a device to protect the park from salt water. Joining the Audubon Society in the action were professional fishing guides and marina operators, as well as two dozen farmers and landowners who feared the effects of intruding salt water on their fields.

Soon the Corps of Engineers and the FCD met with the Audubon Society to work out an agreement. The plug would stay. And not until there was a satisfactory plan to protect the park, would it be removed.

Canal-111 was but one incident in a long chain of problems that had plagued the Everglades. For years the park has stood last in the water line. If heavy rains raised the level of Okeechobee, the Flood Control District, rather than threaten the farmers to the south with too much water, frequently flushed the surplus into the Atlantic through the St. Lucie Canal and westward into the Gulf down the Caloosahatchee. In dry years, farmlands had first claim. Still the National Park scraped along on its inadequate water supplies. Then early in the 1960s, came four years of subnormal rainfall and earth-scorching drought, the worst in a quarter of a century. Several south Florida counties were declared disaster areas. Fires swept the Everglades. Within the park, sloughs and alligator holes dried up. Desperate alligators died while dragging themselves cross-country seeking water. Park naturalists estimated that fully 90 per cent of the park's alligator population perished. So did the minute aquatic creatures which are the beginning of the food chain in the Everglades. Not until the spring of 1966 brought deluges did the drought end. As the National Park was threatened with ruin, people called upon their Congressmen to rescue the Everglades. Congress set the Corps of Engineers to restudying its whole system of water-control structures across south Florida. As one Florida naturalist phrased it, "It's like letting a schoolboy make up his own problems, then grade his own paper."

Not surprisingly, this new study called for more work by the Corps of Engineers. Its scheme for managing water in south Florida, one might assume, had proceeded on long-range planning, soundly built on fine principles of engineering, all tempered with considerations of hydrology and ecology. But in stark fact, the Corps restudy called for $76 million in added funds, mostly for corrective measures.

What had the Engineers originally predicted as the cost of this plan as they moved in with slide rules and power shovels in 1948? According to their own estimates, they could solve south Florida's water troubles at a moderate $208 million. Largely this was to be collected from citizens around the country to benefit Florida developers. By the late 1960s this cost had about doubled. The $76 million corrective topping would bring the cost of the whole layer cake steadily closer to the half-billion dollar mark.

When completed the system will dike, drain, channel, and direct all the water falling in south Florida north of the National Park. More than 2000 miles of levees and canals will stretch like spiderwebs over the River of Grass. Canal-111 is one small link in this drainage system.

Three final points remain to be added to the story of this much-publicized ditch.

On occasion the mighty Corps of Engineers must live with its mistakes. This may be only moderately humbling except in those cases where the evidence is out in public, in view of God and a steady stream of tourists, as was the case with the plug of earth on the site where the conservationists fought the Battle of C-111. It was not precisely the kind of monument the Corps sought. There is good reason to believe that the longer the Engineers looked at that small section of earth the less they could stand the sight of it.

South of the bridge, from which I first viewed the scene, the canal makes a sharp right turn, and its waters are lost from sight. The Corps of Engineers, faced with the need to choose a place for its salt-water intrusion barrier chose to move it down the canal 1500 feet. Here it would be out of sight of the highway. Conservationists insist they might wisely have placed it well up the canal near the plug. Here it would be convenient for workmen. And according to geological studies, it would allow less chance for sea water to percolate through the oölitic limestone around it.

But what of the original reason for enlarging the drainage ditch to a size that would accommodate barge traffic? With the barrier still in place, how world the barges pass? The truth, by this time, was that there was no longer any need for a navigable canal because Aerojet had long since closed its Florida operation. Changes in the space program had put a sudden end to their solid-fuel research and the 75,000 acres lay bleak and abandoned behind locked gates. The added expense of the bigger canal seems wasted. What then was the reason for going ahead and removing the controversial plug from C-111? There was no longer any real reason. No barges would come that way.

According to the Corps of Engineers, their compelling reason for wanting to remove the plug at the earliest moment was to make the ditch perform its drainage work. It would not, they insisted, properly drain the lands north of it as long as that section of earth stopped the water flow. But some people on the scene disagreed with the Engineers on this point too.

Within the National Park Service were hydraulic

engineers and other specialists of long experience watching the waters of south Florida follow the maze of drainage ditches. They pointed to the south side of the canal where half a hundred water gaps built into the wall let surplus waters overflow the canal in periods of heavy runoff. Even with the plug in place, they insisted, those gaps which have plank gates north of C-111, could carry off the surplus water, removing it from the farmlands to the north and spreading it in a broad, flat sheet across the National Park where it was so much needed.

This the Engineers said was ridiculous, and implied that, as engineers, they should know. Handling water was, after all, their specialty. Time and again they said the plug must come out for the canal to do its drainage job. Eventually George B. Hartzog, Jr., Director of the National Park Service, called for help from the hydraulic engineers of the U. S. Geologic Survey. Into the canal went a system of monitoring devices to measure the flow. After weeks of studying and figuring, with the aid of computers, the Geologic Survey concluded that the gaps alone would indeed handle all surplus water from the canal even in the wet months. But the Engineers still wanted that unsightly earthen plug out of there. As long as it was left in place their tidy canal had an unfinished appearance and caused taxpayers to wonder what kind of canal this might be.

In the course of this argument the Corps and the FCD could have removed planks from culverts north of C-111 to let the system work as the Geologic Survey suggested, with the water flowing off into the National Park. But instead, they chose to leave the planks in place and retain water to back upon the lands to the north. Soak those fields enough and the politically powerful landowners were certain to bring pressure to remove the plug. There could have been no other reason.

The Engineers proceeded to move the plug. Early in 1968 the Corps let a contract for building the salt-water control gates down around the bend. The fact that this unneeded engineering structure cost $90,000 worried some local citizens far more than it did the Corps of Engineers. "That's a lot of wasted money," I was told by one professional government employee who asked that his name not be used. "It's more than I will pay into the treasury in income taxes throughout my life."

Eventually, after the Engineers have finished erasing their mistakes and correcting their works, hopefully there will be a realignment of the water distribution across south Florida to assure the National Park a fair supply even in dry years. Lake Okeechobee is being deepened by the construction of the Herbert Hoover Dike, thus providing increased storage capacity. There is agreement that the National Park will be allowed a minimum 315,000 acre-feet of water per year "when practicable."

In 1967 the Regional Director of the U. S. Fish and Wildlife Service wrote a memorandum to the Jacksonville District Office of the Corps of Engineers. What is needed, he insisted, is a shifting in emphasis, ". . . from strict flood control to total water management." This has become self-evident as man has labored to change the character of the Everglades over the years of water manipulation in south Florida.

5. Florida's Scar Tissue

Meanwhile, deep in the heart of Florida, the Corps was engaged in another battle. Again it was their penchant for ditchdigging that brought them unexpected scars from a civilian army, this one led by an irate and cultured lady. What the Engineers proposed to do was go ahead with a cross-Florida barge canal which had been rejected repeatedly for more than 125 years. The canal would connect the Gulf of Mexico with the Atlantic Ocean at a cost of $170 million.

No man can any longer be certain who first had the grand idea that the Peninsula of Florida was eminently suited by virtue of geography to a canal-building venture. It may have occurred even to those earliest explorers who, rounding the peninsula and mapping it as best they could, began to comprehend that this was a thumb sticking out from the mainland. Perhaps some of them even sought a river which connected the ocean on the east with the great gulf on the west. True, some streams did reach inland toward the interior of Florida. But there was no way for ships to cross the peninsula; they could only sail around. Early realization of this geographic fact led to speculation among colonists and politicians. So more than a century and a quarter ago there were serious suggestions that a ship canal be cut across the state.

As early as 1825, the committee on roads and canals of the House of Representatives studied a recommended canal to connect "the waters of the St. Johns with those of the river Suwanee." More than two dozen possible routes were suggested for the canal.

In 1824, during the presidency of James Monroe, canal advocates said this was the answer to speeding the mails between New Orleans and Washington, D.C. Other arguments promised relief from the attacks of pirates and a short cut for sailing vessels to avoid the "dangerous" West Indies. The canal would, it was claimed, ". . . invite emigration to the interior of Florida." All of these arguments have long since been classified as quaint antiques. But down through the years, at least once in each quarter-century this scheme has been repeatedly dusted off and never permitted the quiet death to which logic should long since have consigned it.

Knowledgeable engineers have repeatedly grasped the disadvantages in the concept. Between 1909 and 1911 a party of surveyors worked across Florida studying the feasibility of a canal, as called for in the River and Harbor Act of 1909. The report on the study came in 1913. The essence of this report, which was eventually printed as a House Document of the 63rd Congress, 1st Session, was found in paragraph 3. "The special board discusses fully the probable commercial, naval, and military uses of the canal and it reaches the conclusion that these uses are entirely insufficient to justify the large expenditure then estimated at $15,538,005 required for the construction of the canal and its maintenance, and, therefore, the board is of the opinion that the project is not worthy of being undertaken by the United States." The report was signed by the Chief of Engineers William H. Bixby, United States Army.

In years to come, others in the Corps of Engineers were to reach the same conclusion. In October, 1924, Colonel H. C. Newcomer wrote, "A waterway across the state of Florida of a depth adequate for economical barge service would be very expensive. . . . The Board therefore concurs with the district and division engineers in the view that the provision by the Federal Government of a continuous inland waterway across the State of Florida . . . is not justifiable at the present time."

What had district engineer, Gilbert A. Youngblood, decided that earned this agreement from higher headquarters? ". . . it is my opinion," he said on May 4, 1923, "that the project is not at the present time worthy of adoption by the United States and that a survey is not necessary." Through those years the thinking of the engineers on this project seemed to be in accord with the principles of economics, and they had not yet been forced to weigh the Cross-Florida Barge Canal scheme on the basis of its true pork barrel value to the legislators. This voting-booth justification was to come later.

I was told by one ex-employee of the Corps' Jacksonville office, "We used to have a standing joke around that office. Whenever anyone said he was catching up on his work or finishing a project, somebody would say, 'You can always work on the Cross-Florida Barge Canal.'"

On July 23, 1942 Congress did, at last, authorize construction of the Cross-Florida Barge Canal. Urged on by chambers of commerce across central Florida, and lured by the prospect of solid gold support from politicians, the Corps of Engineers came up with a benefit-cost ratio promising taxpayers of the land slightly more in return than they would plow into the canal. And on this basis they proposed forging ahead.

Their grand plan called for digging a canal 107 miles long to connect the Gulf of Mexico near Yankeetown with the St. Johns River across the state near Palatka. Behind the power shovels would stretch a canal 150 feet wide, with a minimum channel depth of 12 feet. There would be a system of five locks, 84 feet wide and 600 feet long, to lift and lower ships and barges across Florida in stair step stages. Then, to keep the proposed canal supplied with water, the Corps would build two new reservoirs.

More than the length of the canal, it was the proposed route that promptly brought conservation forces into the fray. Long stretches of it would follow the valley of the Oklawaha River, and completely destroy forty-five miles of one of Florida's two remaining truly wild rivers.

Some years ago I first had a water-level look at the Valley of the Oklawaha on a boat trip that began at Silver Springs, largest of Florida's sparkling, natural artesian wells bubbling from the limestone depths of the state. The waters of Silver Springs, after supporting a flotilla of cruising tourists in glass-bottomed boats, flow off through the cypress, tupelo, and live oak trees, down Silver Creek to empty into the Oklawaha. A hundred years ago little steamboats carried tourists along this enchanted stream to the fantastic spring.

Meandering back and forth, following the river's channels through the mile-wide valley, you float on these clean waters through a wooded wilderness that has mysteriously survived the development mania gripping Florida in recent decades. Florida once had other rivers just as wild. But time and man have taken their toll, removed the timber from the valleys, run wastes from pulp mills and citrus plants into the streams, and tamed or ruined the rivers. But not yet the Oklawaha.

There remain across the United States today only a handful of truly wild rivers. In 1961 the Senate Select Committee on National Water Resources set about the task of locating and saving some of these streams.

". . . Their natural scenic, scientific, esthetic and recreational values outweigh their value for water development," said the Committee, "now and in the future."

When the Joint Committee appointed by the Secretaries of Interior and Agriculture listed the sixty-four rivers eligible for the initial wild river study, the Oklawaha was on the list. But between the time the study was completed and the report rendered, the Corps of Engineers had not been idle. The forces proposing the canal that would wreck the Oklawaha knew that the wild river legislation, if permitted to go through, would weaken their case for a barge canal. Economic justification for the project was already shaky and the Engineers feared it could not stand up under further scrutiny or delay. Once dug, and permanently inflicted on the Florida landscape, further argument about its worth would be academic. The politicians advocating the canal hustled about the halls of Congress, and by 1963, the initial appropriations for starting the Cross-Florida Barge Canal in 1964 were firmly implanted in the federal budget. Thus ended any official wild river hope for the Oklawaha.

But it was soon apparent that the Engineers had not heard the last word from those hoping to save this river. Spearheading the counterattack was Marjorie Carr, wife of University of Florida professor Dr. Archie Carr. The uprising began in the Gainesville vicinity with the Alachua Audubon Society. Eventually the campaign would be joined by the Izaak Walton League, the Sierra Club, and hundreds of citizens from across Florida and beyond. I drove one afternoon to the historic village of Micanopy to talk with Mrs. Carr about her battle with the Engineers. It had dragged on for more than two years and looked then like a lost cause.

Pausing only once in the afternoon to point out the

wild otter that lives in the Carrs' private lake, she reviewed for me the long course of the Oklawaha fight with mounting temper. "We knew," she said, "there was no use to try to stop the canal completely. Those who want it are too powerful. All we asked was that they choose an alternate course, a route that would save the forty-five miles of the Oklawaha."

The two planned reservoirs, one behind the Rodman Dam and the other behind the Eureka Dam, were to flood out 27,350 acres of the wild bottom lands. The shallow lakes would become slack water basins from which dense stands of dead tree stumps would protrude. "They asked me," said Mrs. Carr, "where I would make the canal. *They* were asking *me*. I thought this was ridiculous. I took a pencil and drew a line. Just like that! After that they called it 'Mrs. Carr's route.' I think they were a little upset that they hadn't brought it up themselves, but once they make up their minds on a route they are not interested in any alternates. And they defend their choice to the very last."

Mrs. Carr's canal seemed to make better sense than the planned devastation of the river valley. She proposed taking the structure through the sand hills thinly covered with shallow-rooted pines. Here, none of the rich wild lands would be destroyed by flooding the river valley.

But the Corps soon came up with a battery of arguments against it. At first glance the district engineer proclaimed that the uplands through which she advocated taking the canal were too high for economic excavation—some of them 100 feet high. A closer look at the geodetic survey maps revealed, however, that this was an overstatement by at least 25 per cent; nowhere were these hills even 75 feet high.

The conservationists requested the Corps of Engineers to work out a feasibility study of the alternate route through the sand hills. They first hesitated, then complied—after a fashion. Conservationists felt that the Engineers created their "careful study" of the alternate route by sitting in their offices in Jacksonville, and looking at a map of the region. The resulting four page memo declared the alternate route "uneconomical and not feasible." Conservationists began taking the Corps argument apart. The alternate, according to Corps estimates, would add $13,800,000 to the cost of the project. Included here was the anticipated cost for buying 140,000 acres of land. Where were these lands? The Corps was, after all, buying land in the river valley, and here in the alternate route the land lay mostly in the Ocala National Forest, already in government ownership. Several more million dollars were accounted for by the claim that the alternate route would add seven miles to the canal length. This was also difficult for the conservationists to comprehend in view of the fact that the newly proposed route called for twenty-three miles of canal construction instead of the thirty-nine miles in the route planned by the Engineers.

"We are certain," replied the conservation volunteers, "that the Corps' statement that Alternate Route A would increase the project maintenance costs $510,000 annually is an error." Comparing the features of the two routes, they asked, "Is it possible that it will cost more to maintain twenty-three miles of canal and two locks built side by side than it will to maintain thirty-nine miles of canal, 27,000 acres of reservoir and two locks and two dams built in three locations?"

Most of all, the conservation workers objected to the Corps' claim that the alternate route would practically dry up the lower Oklawaha during dry periods. Conspicuously absent from the brief analysis of the alternate route was any provision for keeping water flowing through this alternate canal route. In conversation, and correspondence, the Engineers later agreed with Mrs. Carr that a pumping station could provide this water. Meanwhile, however, the Florida Board of Conservation had given the original route its essential blessing. The Corps' claim that the alternate route threatened to dry up the Oklawaha had done its work.

What the politicians and the Corps of Engineers wanted desperately was to get on with the job. The real need was to get the project moving, get in there and dig, before the objectors brought the whole scheme to a grinding halt. In what must stand as one of the major citizen efforts in recent times to protect the landscape against the attacks of the Engineers, the Alachua Audubon Society, with Mrs. Carr performing much of the work, spread the message widely across the state and beyond.

"We suggest realignment of the canal route from Silver Springs to the St. Johns," they announced, "so the canal will run . . . through the Ocala National Forest, and enter the St. Johns River at the southern end of Lake George. This realigned route to the St. Johns is about ten miles shorter than the present route. Other obvious advantages of the realigned route are 1) reduction of right-of-way costs, 2) reduction of future zoning problems in an area emphasizing out-of-door activities, 3) public access . . . 4) elimination of the future costly and difficult problems of reservoir management."

When the Corps claimed that the alternate route as suggested by Mrs. Carr would dry up the Oklawaha, she asked them if a pumping station might not avert that problem, and if so, what would the cost be? They said that a pumping station to do the job would cost $3,800,000 with a $400,000 annual operating cost. This, at first, seems like a sizable objection to "Mrs. Carr's route," until you realize that this route would eliminate the need for the two planned reservoirs whose combined original cost was estimated by the Corps to be $33.4 million, with an annual maintenance cost of $48,000. It later developed that this projected maintenance figure was likely to be fantastically low. One Corps authority on aquatic weed control admitted privately that the cost of controlling weeds in the impoundments might run more than a million dollars a year. It appears, therefore, that the Corps' official estimate of maintenance costs might have been low by a million dollars a year. An accurate estimate of this cost, of course, would have ruled the project out from the beginning and saved the Oklawaha.

Why then not choose Mrs. Carr's route? The reason is to be found in the recreation benefits claimed for the impoundments. Without including the recreation benefits the project would not qualify. Mrs. Carr's route did not provide for reservoirs. And without the impoundments the Cross-Florida Barge Canal would give up its claim to providing great recreational benefits.

On June 25, 1966, twenty miles east of Ocala, an enthusiastic crowd of canal boosters assembled to wish the Corps Godspeed as it proceeded with its Eureka impoundment, second of the two planned reservoirs. Senator Spessard Holland, "leading promoter of the barge canal," according to a Corps news release, plus assorted lesser politicians and interested parties, partook of the free mullet lunch prepared by the State Board of Conservation.

This "festive occasion," as Corps public relations people called it, was emceed by the president of the Ocala-Marion County Chamber of Commerce. Everyone including the governor was on hand to make brief comments praising the local citizenry on their progressive thinking, and congratulating them on their success in bringing home the grand prize. Said the

Corps news release, "Marion County officials are jubilant over the start of work in Marion County, since nearly $100 million of the total $158 million cost of the canal will be spent in Marion County." Jubilant? Understandably.

The Corps had done its patriotic bit in the spirit of the day. To signal the start of the Eureka project it had brought in sticks of dynamite and used them to shoot puffs of red, white, and blue smoke several hundred feet into the air. Considering that they were thus heralding the obliteration of the cherished Oklawaha River Valley, Mrs. Carr considered this pseudopatriotic display to be, as she wrote Senator Claude Pepper, ". . . an example of extraordinary poor taste."

The conservation forces, which were still being referred to by Lt. General W. F. Cassidy, Chief of the Army Corps of Engineers, as "little old ladies in tennis shoes," had not yet given up the fight for their rare wild river. Repeatedly they had appealed to congressional delegations, only to find government people, from the President down, in solid formation behind the Engineers. The interwoven congressional net which trades support for a project in one electorate for like support in another, refused to yield an inch of ground in Florida.

The Corps of Engineers asked the Federal Water Pollution Control Administration's Southeast Water Laboratory at Athens, Georgia, to study the rivers and report to them. That report was published early in 1967 and it outlined some of the pollution and environmental hazards inherent in the canal. One organism the study group considered is the Asiatic clam, *Corbicula,* an imported pest so far restricted to waters of the Florida Gulf coast. There are sometimes 2000 of them per square foot. By joining the Oklawaha, flowing into the Atlantic, with the Withlacoochee which empties into the Gulf, the Engineers would open an invasion route for this pest to the waters of Florida's Atlantic shore.

Altering the rivers from free-flowing waters to slack-water impoundments would further bring changes in the fish life. As usually happens in new impoundments, the fish could be expected to increase in the first years. But then would come a leveling off and lowering of the populations. Fishermen have long known the clean and fertile free-flowing waters of the Oklawaha as excellent fish producers.

"Mosquitoes and midges will increase," said the report. The slack waters would provide them better living conditions than ever before and the organic materials, instead of being swept downstream on the current, would settle to the bottom to feed the midge larvae.

Then there would be perhaps the biggest problem of all, the water hyacinths. This floating weed with the strikingly beautiful purple flowers is another of Florida's long list of imported plants and animals. Throughout the southeast, this aquatic weed plagues private citizens and government agencies. Mattresses of compacted hyacinths cover entire lakes, cut out the light and eventually damage the fishing. They can make boat travel impossible. Florida has spent great sums moving hyacinths, poisoning them, dredging them, and disposing of them. Slack water and warm climate offer them the environment they need, and the new impoundments on the Oklawaha, according to the pollution specialists, would create what might prove a real boon to the spreading, foreign aquatic weed, and an almost insolvable problem to those charged with keeping the new reservoirs free of such vegetation. "Once established," the report added, "hyacinths have a potential of becoming the dominant aquatic plant . . . water hyacinths are a severe problem because they interfere with most water uses including navigation, fishing, swimming, recreational boating . . ."

How will the authorities deal with the water hyacinths expected to flourish in the new Oklawaha River reservoirs? According to the Federal Water Pollution Control Agency report, they should not use chemicals to kill them. Not only should control be limited to "mechanical means," a staggering physical and financial prospect in itself, but, said the report, the hyacinths should be harvested and hauled away from the lake.

In 1968, Florida's fisheries specialists issued an official commission statement predicting that fishing in the Oklawaha would flourish temporarily following the closing of the dams—perhaps for five to seven years. This is typical of new reservoirs. "During this time," the report then warned, "noxious aquatic weeds are expected to increase as a result of the extremely shallow reservoirs and increasing water fertility." By 1980 the bass fishing will have given way to small sunfish and bullheads, ". . . as the environment becomes less suitable for the production of largemouth bass and chain pickerel." And by 2020, the forecast concluded, even the crappie and channel catfish would be a rare or vanished species within these shallow putrid waters. In their place would live the primitive garfish, mudfish and bullheads. This will be the inheritance of tomorrow's central Florida outdoorsmen. Gradually they will forget what the Oklawaha was like in the days when it flowed free through that wild and productive river bottom.

To those holding out the slender hope that hyacinths would not invade the new waterway, the pollution study offered an alternative scarcely more attractive. Without the hyacinths, they predict dense blooms of blue-green algae which would form mats and windrows and add foul tastes and odors to the waters of the Oklawaha. As the algae die and decay, recreational use of the impounded waters would probably diminish because of what the pollution specialists call "pigpen odors."

In addition to these anticipated troubles, the report foresees that pollution from commercial barge traffic could further damage the Oklawaha with oils, acids, and other wastes.

Sadly, Mrs. Carr told me, "I thought when we started out this would be simple. All it would require, I felt, was to point out a few things to the Corps of Engineers. They would need to understand that the Oklawaha is a treasure, that there is an alternate route and that a lot of people really want the Oklawaha River saved. I thought once these things had been explained to them we could get the canal's course changed. I was naïve," she said.

Incredibly, even as the Engineers dig at the Oklawaha, they already have a Cross-Florida Barge Canal a scant 125 miles to the south. The 155-mile long Okeechobee Waterway, completed by the Corps of Engineers in 1967, was built with a minimum eight-foot channel eighty feet wide. It was complete and open to barge traffic once the Corps had channeled the waters of Lake Okeechobee westward through the Caloosahatchee River to the Gulf of Mexico, and eastward through the St. Lucie Canal to come to the Atlantic Ocean at Stuart. The Federal expenditure on this canal by mid-1968 had totaled $31,181,000.

Citizens of Stuart were elated as the St. Lucie Canal neared completion, sure that it would bring new wealth to their area. Time has told a different story, and many citizens of the area complain of the added load of silt the canal carries into the river's mouth.

The same year the Corps, seeing its Cross-Florida Barge Canal to the north well underway, and apparently judging it safe now to mention the existing canal, prepared to go to Congress with a new plan for the Okeechobee Waterway, initiating a new study to determine the wisdom and cost of enlarging the canal to a minimum 10-foot depth and a 100-foot width. "Actually," said a publication of the Flood Control District, "the Okeechobee Waterway Association is seeking a 12-foot depth and 125-foot width as the minimum . . ."

It has been mildly suggested that the Corps, at a fraction of the cost of the Cross-Florida Barge Canal, could have deepened this existing Okeechobee Waterway to carry heavier traffic and save the Oklawaha. But the Corps did not choose to study the feasibility of such an alternative nor were they legally required to.

This is still not the entire story of Florida's water projects. The list promises to keep the Corps of Engineers busy there throughout the foreseeable future. North of Tampa a big flood-control program calls for a system of eight major impoundments. Then, there is at least one more canal the Engineers hope to scratch across Florida's face. This one is known as "The Missing Link."

When no longer missing, this link will stretch for about two hundred miles down along the Gulf coast, cutting through the tidelands with its deep channel and providing occasional lateral canals through which boats (and the strongest of salt water) can enter the canal. The salt water marshes along this coast are the fertile nurseries for diverse, and ecologically complex, aquatic communities. What a canal cutting through the marshes will do to this aquatic resource is not known. There are two possible locations from which the planners may choose. One would be out in the bay at three feet below the tideline. The other would be dug in the marshes a foot or so above the tideline and be known as the "plus one" route. It would cut through two national wildlife refuges, home of countless water birds, including wintering ducks, and fertile nurseries for fish populations. It is also fully anticipated in some circles that the dredges will slice so deeply into the limestone aquifers beneath the tidelands that salt water will be given free entry into fresh-water sources supplying coastal communities.

The Missing Link would tie into the Cross-Florida Barge Canal. Each one is essential to the other when the Engineers get down to proving that their works are economically justified. The Missing Link connects with the Cross-Florida Barge Canal, and the Cross-Florida Barge Canal (understandably) connects with the Missing Link.

Where does it end in Florida? Where does Florida end? With new canals slicing the peninsula into sections, new lakes in a land of lakes, new building developments for the climbing population, mangrove swamps bulldozed and filled, bays dredged, wetlands drained and forests scalped, progress reigns supreme. Soon all of Florida will be "improved," not by any over-all plan, but by bits and pieces. And once completely "improved," this land of sunshine and balmy breezes will have had its face lifted in a surgical technique so drastic that the ages will inherit the scar tissue.

6. The Biggest Dam

Across the heart of Alaska the Yukon River lies like a giant half-moon. It rises in the wild mountains of Canada's Yukon territory, flows northward into Alaska, then turns south to meander toward the Bering Sea, two thousand miles from its beginning.

Along the way, it picks up volume from its tributaries and near the middle of its course reaches the Yukon Flats. Here, for two hundred miles, it wanders restlessly over the valley which, in places, is eighty miles wide. As spring warms the air, melting snows fatten the Yukon until there is an irresistible pressure against the icy lid with which winter capped the river. The water rises and the rotting ice groans and creaks. No longer able to restrain the swelling river in its bed, the layer of ice cracks, breaks, and piles up along its course until its shimmering edges rise like giant blades. Grinding against itself, and everything in its path, the ice gouges new routes for the Yukon across this wide valley.

Abandoned channels become oxbow lakes which over the years will be hidden beneath the sediment and the green vegetation. If you fly over the Yukon, you see the evidence of this ever-changing landscape of potholes, lakes, and sloughs. The patches of willow, which may grow ten feet high and which provide feed for the moose during the bitter winter, mark the areas recently cleared by ice. Then, gradually, the fragile aspen invade the willow stands only to be replaced during the following years by the spruce which grows eventually into pure stands, forming dark-green patches across the Yukon Flats.

But each spring brings its changes. As the flowing ice clears parts of the old timber stands, the vegetative pattern is rejuvenated. These changes keep the Flats growing new crops of willows for the moose, and create new shallow wetlands where waterfowl congregate to nest. It is one of the far north's most productive wildlife regions, kept youthful and vigorous by the free-flowing Yukon. After crossing the Yukon Flats, the river approaches the Rampart Canyon where rock walls set its course.

Near here, on a dark and bitterly cold day late one February there came, mingling with the whine of the snow-laden north wind, the foreign moans of hard-laboring vehicles. For several days the airplanes came with their cargoes of machinery, fuel, and food, to land on a ready-made airstrip of river ice. A ten-man crew erected four metal huts in which to live. Then some of them drove off across the crusted snow with those huge drills they had hauled from Fairbanks.

The whining drills pushed deep into the frozen earth and the bedrock below. This exploratory effort was an early step in a fantastic scheme to block the fourth largest river in North America with a towering concrete dam and create the largest lake ever built by man.

Imaginative engineers had dreamed of it for years. By damming this river in the Far North they would erect in artificial stone, an everlasting monument to their skill as dam builders. And it had suddenly begun to look as if the dollars needed for the monstrous dam would soon begin flowing northward from that bubbling tax fountain on the banks of the far-away Potomac.

The dam which the Corps of Engineers proposed

to build would rise 530 feet above bedrock and stretch 4700 feet across the valley. In spite of the Yukon's volume, the new reservoir behind this dam would not be completely filled for at least twenty years.

But once it had reached its full size, the reservoir would be larger than Lake Erie. It would cover an area greater than the state of New Jersey.

First estimates, in 1964, placed the possible cost at $1.2 billion, to be paid by taxpayers from all parts of the United States. The Corps of Engineers had said nothing about how rising construction costs might alter this figure during the building time of possibly ten years. An outside study group later adjusted the cost estimate to a minimum of $2 billion.

For this treasure, Alaska would be handed a desolate wind-swept inland sea two hundred and eighty miles long, and eighty miles wide. Beneath the massive weight of its waters would be the age-old range of the moose, and the nesting grounds where a million waterfowl are produced annually. The value of these wildlife resources would eventually figure into the fate of the giant project. The lake would also cover the ancestral homes and hunting and fishing grounds of 1200 Athabascan Indians living in scattered settlements along the river.

To follow the sequence of power plays leading up to 1964 takes one along a circuitous and sometimes obscure trail. Since 1954 the Corps of Engineers had been working out details of a plan for power development along the Yukon and Kuskokwim rivers. The Rampart scheme began to intrigue some Corps officials increasingly. Then shortly after Alaska attained statehood, the Senate Public Works Committee, urged on by Alaska's delegation, asked the Corps of Engineers to investigate and report on the possibilities of constructing a dam at Rampart Canyon on the Yukon. When the Alaska Rural Electric Cooperative Association met for its eighth annual session in Fairbanks in August, 1959, Harold L. Moats, Chief of the Civil Works Planning Branch of the Alaska District Office, Corps of Engineers, delivered an inspiring message. Until then, he said, there had been a lot of talk about Rampart but nothing accomplished. "Rampart Canyon, the big one," he promised, "is Alaska's most valuable resource, and as it is developed, Alaska will take her rightful place in the family of states contributing richly to the economy of the nation and to the welfare of the whole free world."

With each such utterance the hopes of Alaskans rose. The future was all blue sky, big water—and big money.

As the drama unfolded, the Corps had second thoughts about ideas it had already committed to writing. Beginning in 1948, on authority of the Flood Control Act of that year, Corps workers had prepared a series of at least seven *Interim Reports* exploring the potentials in Alaska for hydroelectric plants as well as flood control and various navigation structures. What they recommended was a succession of smaller hydroelectric plants designed to meet the needs of developing communities over the coming decades. But the Corps of Engineers suddenly changed direction in 1959 and disregarded these earlier recommendations for small power plants.

The *Interim Report* Number Seven, to have been published in 1959, finally was ready in 1964. Early drafts of that report are, understandably, no longer available. But an Alaskan who studied one draft critically recalls its flat conclusion that no hydroelectric project on the Yukon was considered feasible for recommendation at that time by the Corps of Engineers.

The intervening years between the first and final drafts of the *Interim Report* Number Seven were filled with intrigue, infighting, and power politics. The Corps of Engineers decided that maybe there was some reason for recommending a power plant on the Yukon, in spite of earlier thinking. *Interim Report* Number Seven, finally printed as House Document No. 218, 88th Congress, Second Session, said, "The District Engineer recommends that the potential projects reported on herein be adopted as a basis for further investigations to meet the future needs for developing the water resources in the Yukon and Kuskokwim basins."

What had prompted this one hundred and eighty degree turnaround in Corps thinking? The events up to this point shed considerable light on the manner in which some of our massive dams are conceived.

When Alaska became the largest but most thinly populated state in 1959, political leaders there knew at once that they would face an urgent need for money. The price of running the new state government, estimated at $20 million for the first year, actually came to $36 million, then rose to $46 million for the second year, and $56 million the third year. Meanwhile the infusion of federal military funds into Alaska was diminishing. Taxes were increasingly burdensome. In light of these circumstances the promise of several billion dollars, spent at Rampart Canyon over a decade, was a glittering solution to many problems.

Alaska's former Senator, Ernest Gruening, had scarcely reached the Washington scene before he began stumping for the gigantic reservoir on the Yukon. Russia, it appeared, threatened to outdistance the United States in the kilowatt race, and power is a basic building block in the total economic growth of any country. Soon the senate "instructed" its Committee on Public Works to investigate the possibilities of keeping ahead in the power race. One of the results was an inspection trip to the U.S.S.R. by Senate members of the Committee on Interior and Insular Affairs. The party included Senators Moss of Utah, Muskie of Maine, and Ernest Gruening of Alaska. Senator Gruening knew that building the great Yukon impoundment in his state would put the United States ahead. Here was a salable idea: the "patriotic" thing to do was to build Rampart. Back in Washington, Senator Gruening hit the Yukon trail with more vigor than anyone since the gold-rush days. Meanwhile, the Corps of Engineers, waiting discreetly on the sidelines, was sitting tight on *Interim Report* Number Seven.

During hearings on Alaska's hydroelectric needs, Senator Gruening had the opportunity to report the conclusions of his studies and his trip to Russia. He insisted that construction on Rampart Dam should be expedited. Two months later the Alaska State Legislature put through a resolution urging the United States Government to get on with it and build Rampart Dam as soon as possible.

Strangely enough, Senator Gruening landed a spot as chairman of the Senate Subcommittee on Irrigation and Reclamation of the Committee of Interior and Insular Affairs. In that capacity he was "directed" by the regular committee chairman to investigate Alaska's hydroelectric needs, and shortly afterward, he was off to Alaska on a series of official one-man hearings. These occasioned some forceful stumping for his favorite reservoir-in-waiting. Gathered with him at the "hearings," were members of Chambers of Commerce from around the state, representatives of the power industry, even the governor himself—all enthusiastically endorsing the plan to flood out 10,200 square miles of their state.

Meanwhile the farsighted Corps of Engineers, looking ahead to the possibilities of future criticism, was further insulating itself in its own position. One of its moves was to appoint an outside consulting firm to determine whether or not there was indeed a market for the power Rampart might eventually produce. The firm chosen for this assignment had a staff top-heavy with big-power advocates, including ex-TVA policymakers.

Early in 1961 the Corps also set up an advisory board. Senator Gruening duly noted the fact by reading the announcement into the Congressional Record. Within the next year this group was to assemble on three occasions, and discuss the various economic aspects of the proposed dam, ranging from sale of power to dead ducks. And in the process it would bring out some of the more interesting conflicts of interest revolving around the Rampart controversy.

Throughout most of the three lengthy hearings of the Rampart Economic Advisory Committee there was no mention of what the new lake—the biggest lake man had ever constructed—would be named. To some, such as Committee member Stanley J. McCutcheon, there seemed but one choice. During a meeting late in March 1962, he asked the representative of the U. S. Fish and Wildlife Service, "Mr. Watson, have you been able to estimate the loss of wild fowl that would result from flooding caused by Gruening Lake?"

In those early years any Alaskan citizens who openly opposed the Rampart scheme risked condemnation as the Benedict Arnolds of the Far North. Alaskan politicians could no more afford to be against Rampart than they could risk belittling motherhood. The great concrete cornucopia promised to spill the good things of life over Alaskans ever after, and sobering second thoughts were not welcomed. State politicians who dared voice their doubts about Rampart lost elections. State game and fish workers, some of whom were against the Rampart idea, were muzzled. When a faculty member of the University of Alaska questioned the wisdom of building the dam, a member of the Alaskan House of Representatives spoke of cutting university appropriations.

Advocates of Rampart even resented delays essential to searching out more detailed facts about the dam and the demand for its power. Their fears were justified. The longer and more critically Rampart was examined, the less attractive it began to look. Perhaps few developments frustrated the dam advocates more than the stream of statistics that began to emerge from studies of the U. S. Fish and Wildlife Service.

By legislative directive the Corps of Engineers is obligated to consider the effects of its projects on the wildlife resources of the area under question. This segment of the investigation falls upon the biologists of the U. S. Fish and Wildlife Service. Their report becomes part of the final plan presented to Congress by the Corps, and is available when the project is considered for funding. It was one thing for the Corps to find that the dam could be successfully built, quite another to prove that it should be.

Gordon Watson, a youthful biologist who had lived in Alaska since 1952, was responsible for the Fish and Wildlife Service investigation. He had represented the Fish and Wildlife Service on the Advisory Committee and sat through all three meetings of that group. From the first, some committee members were openly antagonistic toward Watson, as the representative of the Fish and Wildlife Service.

A wildlife census revealed that the area under consideration is home to about 12,000 moose. The willows, sometimes ten feet tall, provide them an ideal winter food source, when other vegetation is unavailable. What is to keep moose from moving out of the Flats ahead of the rising water and relocating in the hills above the lake? The answer to this frequent question is well known to ecologists. If the hills around the Flats could support greater populations of moose, they would already be living there. Moose have, through the ages, increased to the full carrying capacity of the land. The same answer applies to those who wonder why the waterfowl that would be flooded out of the Flats by the planned dam could not live elsewhere in Alaska.

The loss of waterfowl resulting from flooding the Yukon Flats would be staggering. Gordon Watson and his co-workers found that the duck population during the summer nesting season is about fifty ducks per square mile, an extremely high population for Alaska. There are pintails, widgeon, scaup, mallards, and some others. Banding studies soon proved that these Yukon-grown ducks spread into all four major waterfowl flyways, although most of them travel southward into California and some go on into Mexico. Canvasbacks produced in the Yukon Flats account for 9 per cent of the continental population of this species. Taken together, the waterfowl coming south each year from the Yukon Flats comes to 1.5 million—more than the annual production in all the national wildlife refuges set aside since 1903.

Long-legged, dingy-colored sandhill cranes seek out these Flats for their nests too. About ten thousand cranes nest where the lake would stand. And they have as neighbors, ten thousand geese.

In addition to these living sacrifices, investigators explained that below the dam, the Yukon, tamed by the lake and denied its periodic flooding, would gradually become less and less suitable for wildlife.

There were other wild creatures to consider: bears, caribou, muskrats, mink, beaver, otters, wolverine, marten, and foxes, as well as the species with which men are not often directly concerned, including the ravens, gulls, and songbirds.

Then there were the fish, especially the famed salmon which migrate from the sea up the Yukon each year to spawn. This is one of the largest known spawning runs made by anadromous fish anywhere in the world. Of all the salmon traveling the Yukon, the chinook, choice food for humans, makes the longest trip. But the chum and coho salmon travel almost as far. These trips take some of them far beyond the Ramparts and the dam site. From its netting and tagging studies, the Fish and Wildlife Service computed that the salmon migrating beyond the dam site total 20,000 chinook, 50,000 coho and 200,000 chum. Even with devices for lifting these migrants over the dam, it was believed by the biologists that the fish would never find their way beyond the sprawling waters of the giant lake.

Compared with civilian forces beating the drums in behalf of the project, the sedate Corps of Engineers worked from the side lines, well-mannered, and slightly aloof from the ground-level skirmishes. If there is one field in which the Corps excels, in addition to concrete pouring, it is wending its way unscratched through tricky political jungles. Granted its usual caution, plus a smattering of luck, the Corps could come out of this ruckus with no egg on its face at all.

In October, 1963, Rampart partisans increasingly concerned about the fate of their cherished plum, organized a group of citizens into a promotion society to speak up everywhere for Rampart Dam. They called their group "Yukon Power For America, Inc." At least five of its leaders had been members of the late Rampart Economic Advisory Board, which had now completed its tasks and been disbanded by the Corps of Engineers. From Anchorage and Fairbanks city treasuries came $10,000 for use by Y.P.A. Mayor George Sharrock of Anchorage called a big public conference at Mt. McKinley National Park for September of that year, to plan a campaign that would help sell the idea to Congressmen from other sections of the country. Attending the McKinley meeting were nine former members of the Corps' advisory board.

By this time the Rampart controversy was spreading to every state, and the bothersome conservation forces were now fully alerted. Waterfowl hunters, naturalists, and outdoorsmen in general were indignantly pointing at weaknesses in the Rampart scheme. How sincere they really were about the threat of Rampart was to be tested in 1964.

According to Senator Gruening these troubles with what he called "conservation extremists" all started at once. "And then, all of a sudden, out of the blue," he said, "came an attack without warning; an attack completely unexpected." He referred to a speech made by one of the most eminent of all modern wildlife conservationists, Dr. Ira N. Gabrielson of the Wildlife Management Institute.

Speaking in Detroit at the twenty-eighth North American Wildlife and Natural Resources Conference early in 1963, Dr. Gabrielson had said, among other things, that a very determined effort was being made to rush Ramparts authorization through Congress. "Rampart Dam," he added, "is synonymous with resources destruction."

The following month a new element was introduced to the Rampart battle by Terry Brady, an articulate reporter who in his articles for the Fairbanks *News-Miner*, had attempted to show both sides of the issue. An Alaskan with a nose for history had mentioned to Brady a ninety-two-year-old treaty that so far had escaped public notice. The Treaty of Washington, proclaimed July 4, 1871, stated that, "The navigation of the River Yukon . . . , ascending and descending from, to and into the sea, shall forever remain free and open for the purposes of commerce to the subjects of the Britannic majesty . . ." In spite of the fact that Rampart advocates seemed to see no international complications, many Canadians viewed it differently. Among them, no doubt, were those native Canadians whose livelihood depended upon Yukon River salmon caught upriver from the Alaskan border.

That phase of the Rampart study involving the fate of wildlife along the Yukon filled growing amounts of space in newspapers and magazines across the country. Some Congressmen probed with increasingly penetrating questions. Some entered evidence against the project into the Congressional Record. With this much attention on Rampart it was not surprising that conservation organizations should pool their resources to seek the truth about the cost in wildlife.

The Natural Resources Council of America is a top-level co-ordinating body with representatives from such diverse conservation organizations as the Boone and Crockett Club, Defenders of Wildlife, Sierra Club, Wildlife Society, and the Duck Hunters Association of California. A total of fifteen civilian organizations pooled $25,000 for one more special study, which would review all pertinent studies related to Rampart. Their six-man study team was headed by Dr. Stephen H. Spurr of the University of Michigan. Dr. Spurr had some definite ideas about the approach their new study should take. "It would not be enough," he said, "to find out what would not work. This should be a constructive report on how Alaska's resources might be utilized best. One of Dr. Spurr's early moves was to speak with the Corps of Engineers. Would they be willing to accept the findings of his special study committee? Convinced perhaps that no group would make the project look less attractive, the Corps quickly offered its approval.

Rampart's advocates were reeling from the recent figures which wildlife biologists had advanced as the cost of replacing some of the wildlife which would be sacrificed by the dam. The Fish and Wildlife Service, under law, suggests plans intended to mitigate losses of wildlife in Corps of Engineer projects. There would be an annual loss of 1.5 million ducks, 12,800 geese, 10,000 cranes, 20,000 grebes, 13,000 moose, 3.6 million commercial fur bearers, and perhaps 400,000 salmon. The Fish and Wildlife Service biologists did not even attempt to translate these losses into terms of dollars. Such an exercise in arithmetic would almost certainly have rendered it impossible for the Corps to come up with a respectable benefit-cost ratio on Rampart. What the biologists did complete was a study on how the anticipated wildlife losses might be mitigated. To replace only 20 per cent of the lost waterfowl, by such measures as building duck-production ponds around the reservoir, and provide for a minor number of the fur-bearing animals Rampart would sacrifice, would cost $636 million plus $10 million annually for operation of the structures. Even then it was viewed as a gamble.

What did Senator Gruening think of these findings? Briefly, he declared them biased and extreme opinions of dickey birders and moose lovers, a charge which led Secretary Udall to seek the advice of a group outside either camp. He turned to the impartial and respected National Academy of Science. Their report back to the Secretary said that considering the size of the area, time involved, and money allotted, the Fish and Wildlife Service had done an excellent job. Their major objection was that the Fish and Wildlife Service, if anything, was underestimating the losses. Dr. Spurr's group of half a dozen famed ecologists and economists labeled the Fish and Wildlife Service findings "conservative."

With all of the studies completed and the committee reports assembled, former Secretary of the Interior

Stewart L. Udall was faced with making his department's recommendations on whether to build Rampart Dam or not to build. Published in mid-1967, his report dealt the final blow to the fantastic dream plan of Senator Gruening and the Corps of Engineers for the Yukon.

Secretary Udall's authority for bringing the Rampart scheme to a standstill is to be found in a March 14, 1962, letter of agreement between the Secretaries of the Army and the Department of the Interior, and the Provisions of the Fish and Wildlife Conservation Act. The Act called upon the Corps to study the possible effects of the project on fish and wildlife. The letter of agreement divided the areas of investigation between the Army and Interior. As a result of this study, Secretary Udall's report recommended against Rampart.

The report reviewed the conclusions of the study groups, and the early claims of Rampart's benefits began to slide from view behind a barrage of facts. Rampart could produce thirty times as much power as currently used by Alaska's southeast and Railbelt Areas. There was serious question that the great amounts of power produced would find a market. A series of smaller projects was recommended instead. As for the wildlife, Dr. Spurr's committee had said, "Construction of the dam would destroy a highly productive area which is presently benefiting the whole of North America at no cost." Timber, navigation, power, treaties, and over-all economics, all were discussed.

And at the same time that the Rampart forces had been busiest extolling the dollar benefits of their gigantic structure, the shadow of the uranium atom was looming larger and darker over the picture. Nuclear power was a youthful and vigorous newcomer to the power industry.

This was detailed in the News Bulletin of the Alaska Conservation Society, by Dan Swift who punched one more hole in the proposed dam. Swift compared the cost of kilowatts derived from Rampart with those that might come from nuclear power plants. He pointed out that the anticipated $1.3 billion cost of the project made the capital investment for 4.7 million kilowatts come to $276 per kilowatt. Meanwhile, General Electric was then quoting a price of $103 million for a nuclear plant capable of turning out one million kilowatts—or less than half the cost of power that would be generated by Rampart. Since then the competitive position of atomic power versus hydroelectric power has improved steadily.

The trend toward use of atomic power had begun gaining momentum seriously around 1960. The United States Atomic Energy Commission foresaw nuclear power as economically competitive with fossil-fueled power plants by 1968. It is now history that atomic power became competitive even faster than the AEC anticipated. While there were sixteen such plants in operation in 1967, there were another sixty-seven in various stages of planning or construction—an increase that would bring the total power produced by nuclear fission from three million kilowatts to 53 million. By 1968, one-half of the new plants being constructed were designed for nuclear power.

Speaking at Holy Cross University in June, 1964, President Lyndon B. Johnson announced, "In the past several months we have achieved an economic breakthrough in the use of large-scale reactors for commercial power. As a result of this rapid progress we are years ahead." If construction on the Rampart Dam had begun as early as 1965, the project would not have been producing full power for thirty years. The AEC predicts that by then most new power installations will be atomic plants.

Discussing the lack of a market for the annual production of thirty-four billion kilowatts which the installation would eventually generate, the report of Dr. Spurr's committee called Rampart, ". . . the most expensive gamble ever suggested in hydroelectric development—and there is little evidence on hand to indicate that the probability of success is high." This struck to the heart of the question. By civil engineering standards there could be no doubt that Rampart Canyon is a good location for a dam. But why dam the river if the electric power could not be economically marketed as it became available? "Rampart is a 'cathedral' project," Dr. Spurr's committee concluded, "an all-or-nothing venture. One cannot dam half the Yukon."

Behind the final negative decision on Rampart may also have been a Canadian opinion stronger than many Rampart advocates realized. In its October 30, 1967 issue, the *Financial Times of Canada* ran a story dealing with Rampart in which it stated, "The word went out unofficially that if all else failed, Canada would probably deny access for the lines, forcing the U.S. to go into the expensive and chancy business of submarine transmission. At this point the U. S. Government had second thoughts."

Some conservation workers have openly stated that Rampart is dead. But as late as May, 1967, Senator Gruening caused to be inserted in the Congressional Record evidence of unwavering determination to see the Yukon dammed with concrete. He considered Rampart still alive like a slumbering giant, that would awaken at some future moment. The ending of this Rip Van Winkle stage, he implied, might come with the replacement of certain government workers whose tenure on the scene must be considered transitory. "Unfortunately," he said, "the plans for Rampart have been delayed and hindered by uninformed and prejudiced criticisms of certain of my fellow conservationists who I believe may be described as extremists . . .

"However it is necessary to recognize the existence of those powerful special interests represented by certain conservation groups opposing this marvelous project. They have captured the support of the Secretary of the Interior who informed me over the phone some weeks ago that his department would report adversely on Rampart . . . However, this is a Corps of Engineers project, to which Congress entrusted its responsibility, and while the opposition of this Secretary of the Interior is to be regretted, it need not be fatal . . . Meanwhile, despite the attacks on Rampart, Alaskans continue to work for construction of this dam and are confident it will be built." Later in 1968, ironically, Senator Gruening lost the senatorial nomination in a primary election and was himself out of the Senate.

Meanwhile, Alaska's Governor Walter J. Hickel was among those still dreaming of a day when the giant dam would span the Yukon Canyon. "It will take work," he told me, "to convince conservationists that the dam would really not be bad for wildlife."

During a visit to Alaska in the summer of 1968 I heard it rumored that if Richard Nixon were elected President, Governor Hickel would be his choice for Secretary of the Interior. To conservationists this possibility seemed too fantastic to deserve serious attention. The governor's record of resource exploitation and his emphasis on economic development at any cost was well known.

The furor that arose around the new President's announcement, following the November elections, that Hickel was indeed his choice for Secretary of the Interior, may have put the brakes on some of the projects Secretary Hickel hoped to set in motion. I felt certain, from having talked with him, that the

Rampart Dam would get his early attention. In his new office he controlled the department which had effectively blocked the dam across the Yukon. The stage was now set for Alaskans to ask the Corps of Engineers to reappraise once more the feasibility of a Rampart Canyon dam. It is a long way from dead.

7. Closer to God Courtesy Bureau of Reclamation

On a brilliant autumn day several years ago, I drove across the Yellowstone River not far from where it joins the Missouri in western North Dakota. Turning south I followed the river valley through the border town of Fairview and down to the bustling agricultural center of Sidney, Montana, which has a story to tell.

At the turn of the century, the thirsty ranches of this valley were watered only by the annual 15-inch precipitation. Tough, resourceful range cattle were spread thinly over the dry hills. But in the broad bottomlands along the river valley, the dark soil was fertile. The Yellowstone rises in the mountains of Yellowstone National Park several hundred miles to the southwest. It flows past Billings, Miles City, Glendive, and on to Sidney. It was here in this valley of the Lower Yellowstone that the infant Reclamation Service decided to start one of its first federal water management projects.

Congress had in mind precisely such dry but promising lands in 1902 when it created the Reclamation Service, which later became the Bureau of Reclamation within the Department of the Interior. By 1904, reclamation workers were busy along the Lower Yellowstone, scratching away at the dry hills and valleys. With long-handled shovels and horse-drawn scoops they cut 75 miles of canals and 250 miles of lateral irrigation ditches. Across the Yellowstone River they constructed a modest dam to impound waters to feed the canals. The dam, standing but nine and a half feet above the river channel, scarcely changed the contours of the stream and the fertile river bottom lands were not flooded.

The anticipated cost of the Lower Yellowstone project—$4,125,654—was by today's standards modest indeed. In the spring of 1909 the network of canals was completed. The system today waters some 60,000 acres throughout 72 miles of the valley. Water brought new economy. Sugar beets became the major cash crop. Each September, long lines of heavily loaded trucks move them to the mill in Sidney. Sidney has also become a major livestock-marketing center. Logically, the new Bureau of Reclamation was moving into those tasks that seemed best suited to its assignment. A prominent farmer in the valley told me, "This is one of the best projects the Bureau of Reclamation ever built." And most people seem to agree.

If the Bureau had been content to restrict its activities to such valleys, and such tasks as Congress originally intended for it, the chances are good that it would have earned considerably less criticism than it has in recent times. But over the years its scope has changed dramatically, until in some regards it ranks with its competitor the Army Corps of Engineers in the rush to inflict its works on the western states. Today the Bureau, with about 11,000 workers, operates in seventeen western states, Alaska, and Hawaii. The commissioner's office is in Washington, D.C., the chief engineer is in Denver, and offices are scattered through seven regions and many project areas.

The earliest irrigation systems built in the west were constructed not by the government but by private interests. In 1832, irrigation waters began to flow through open ditches to gardens along the Arkansas River in Colorado. In Utah, in 1848, the Mormons employed irrigation on a larger scale. There followed other irrigation systems—especially in Colorado and California—all paid for by private interests. Inevitably, the lands best situated for sound, economic irrigation development were being claimed and developed. By the turn of the century most such places had already been claimed. Then developers began turning their eyes increasingly toward the government. The only question seemed to be one of whether the state government or the federal government should shoulder the burden.

Here again, it was not the farmers seeking aid as much as the business community. Manufacturers and representatives of the big railroads organized the National Irrigation Association in 1899, and by the following year this group was actively pressuring the government to acquire all the available reservoir sites, as well as rights to the waters to fill them. The association changed its name to the National Reclamation Association, still a powerful force when the Bureau of Reclamation needs influence in Congress.

The Reclamation Act of 1902 established the Reclamation Service which became the Bureau of Reclamation in 1923. During its first decade of life, 97 per cent of the Bureau's efforts were devoted to developing irrigation. Today that original assignment accounts for only about one-third of its efforts. Now this Bureau claims such benefits as navigation, flood control, fish and wildlife enhancement, power production, recreation, and water supplies for industries and municipalities.

By its own calculations the Bureau of Reclamation has now impounded enough water to flood the state of New York to a depth of four feet. By 1967 these waters were backed up behind 252 dams throughout the west. At the same time the Bureau had erected forty-eight power plants with a combined capacity of

6.9 million kilowatts, and was riding herd on some 15,000 miles of high-voltage lines. Its 344 canals had a combined length of 6781 miles. One of its most frequent claims, and a tenet which its calls, "A fundamental feature of the Reclamation Program," is "that to a large extent, the direct beneficiaries of a project pay for it." This cherished ideal deserves a closer look.

As originally conceived, Reclamation was to construct largely self-liquidating projects. Those who used the irrigation waters would have ten years in which to repay the government investment. From the beginning the government agreed to subsidize these projects by paying the interest on them. It still does. Soon it became apparent that the newly formed irrigation districts would be unable to repay the cost of the systems within the allotted decade. In 1914 Congress rewrote the rules for the Bureau of Reclamation and doubled the payment period. In 1926 it was doubled again to make the pay-back time forty years. In 1939 an additional ten years was added by a law stating that the repayment did not have to start until ten years after project completion. Now the repayment time was fifty years.

Even then, few such projects have repaid their costs. Contracts have frequently been rewritten to allow extensions, with the taxpayers meanwhile continuing to pick up the tab for the interest. The interest rate is generally a not very realistic 2½ per cent. But even so, as economist Otto Eckstein has made clear in his excellent book, *Water Resources Development*, this interest rate nearly doubles the cost of a Reclamation project, providing it is paid back in the prescribed half century.

The Bureau of Reclamation frequently contends that the interest on its projects is paid for, not by the taxpayer, but from such sources as the sale of power from its generating plants. Careful studies have made this claim also appear shaky. As analyzed by Dr. Eckstein, Bureau of Reclamation power rates just about cover the cost of the power investment with interest, leaving little if anything to repay irrigation system costs.

Even the "good" projects to which the Bureau of Reclamation points with pride have had their financial troubles. Some years ago they selected seven such irrigation districts, then computed the added income taxes the government collects as a result of these irrigation systems. Next they pointed out that the tax increases surpassed the cost of the projects. Therefore the nation was getting its money's worth. One of these projects was the Lower Yellowstone Project. But by January 1, 1968, sixty-four years after the project started, the district still owed the United States Government $251,996.74.

In 1920 and 1939 acts of Congress bolstered the faltering reclamation funds by funneling into them portions of the monies collected from the Mineral Oil Leasing Act, the naval oil reserves, and electric power produced at reclamation dams.

Where a reclamation project can also claim benefits from flood protection, it is all to the good because flood protection is non-reimbursable. Other non-reimbursable benefits claimed include navigation and recreation.

More or less typical of Bureau of Reclamation projects today is the sad and costly case of surgery and face lifting along the famed Big Hole River in Montana. When I last visited this magnificent stream, it was with a sense of sadness because the Big Hole was being ushered into its final days as a free-flowing western river.

Follow the Big Hole River to its beginnings and you come to the mountain snowfields along the Continental Divide. Here in the headwaters, streams, created by melting snows, feed cold water down through the broad Big Hole Valley, forty miles long and five miles wide, a land which natives like to call their "valley of 10,000 haystacks." Tiny sparkling ice water creeks flowing through the upper reaches of the Big Hole still support populations of the disappearing Montana grayling. From this valley where the fabled Chief Joseph made his stand, comes the Big Hole River gathering cold waters from such tributary creeks as Pintlar and Grasshopper, until it reaches the village of Divide. This is where the Big Hole starts for visiting fishermen. In these lower reaches, waters of the Big Hole slide around boulders, rush against red rock cliffs, and wash over riffles to pick up fresh supplies of oxygen before dropping into quiet pools to flow between rows of cottonwoods. The fifty-one miles of the Big Hole to its junction with the Jefferson River has long been listed by Montana as one of its official Blue Ribbon Trout Streams.

There is one place in the Big Hole Valley that, more than all others, was destined to arouse the dam-building instincts of the engineers. Seventeen miles above the river's mouth in the Reichle area, the stream is flanked on both sides by towering cactus-strewn hills that pinch in close to its banks. Such a narrow pass cries out to be dammed. Such free-flowing water challenges those who know how to hold it back in great sluggish basins.

For many years the Bureau of Reclamation had looked with longing on this valley. Their dream was to divert irrigation water to 64,210 acres of ranchland in the Jefferson-Whitehall area downstream near the confluence of the Jefferson, Gallatin, and Madison rivers where the fabled Missouri is created. One of their earliest plans for carrying water to these arid lands was advanced in the early 1940s. This scheme would have taken water from both the Big Hole and the Madison rivers. But it was so effectively fought by local sportsmen that for several years the Bureau of Reclamation let the issue simmer down.

Meanwhile, business interests around the agricultural center of Townsend never forgot the plan, nor for that matter did the Bureau of Reclamation. The Big Hole River seemed a small enough price to pay for added sales of fertilizer and machinery. To Townsend businessmen anyone standing in the way of the Reichle Dam, was against progress. Even without turning to their adding machines, they could visualize the staggering influx of federal money soon to bolster their local economy. In one public meeting, an opponent of the damming of the Big Hole dared asked a Townsend farmer how much he wanted for nothing. The answer, straight from the hip, was "As much as I can get."

Ingeniously, the engineers plan not to use the Big Hole waters near their source. They will move them instead more than a hundred miles through a tediously engineered system of canals, ditches, and siphons, delivering them downstream to portions of the Jefferson and Missouri river valleys where gravity and Mother Nature would eventually take them anyhow. Asked the obvious question as to why it would not be better to build the impoundment downsteam, closer to the area to be irrigated, saving the free-running Big Hole, the engineers had a ready answer. The valley of the Jefferson is wide and a reservoir there would be costly, and would cover up more valuable farmland than it would in the Big Hole country. The maze of canals designed for the job will begin on the Big Hole eight miles below the dam. Water diverted from the river into this ditch will snake around the hills for forty-six miles to the Whitehall neighboorhood, where ranches will spread it over 10,230 acres. Downstream from this canal will be a second one to draw off water enough to irrigate 53,980 additional acres in the Jefferson area.

Interesting from more than one point of view is the Bureau's claim that the alternative plans would be too expensive. First is the question of what the project as planned will actually cost. The total cost of building this project was listed by the Bureau as $82.2 million. The Bureau is permitted to charge off against this investment a number of presumed benefits other than irrigation. Even after figuring all the imaginable benefits to which it was entitled, the Bureau's plan still looked economically soft. The U. S. Fish and Wildlife Service said the wildlife benefits would come to $178,535 per year. The Director of the Montana Game and Fish Department summed up his reaction to this in a single word, "absurd." He pointed out that we are rapidly getting new reservoirs and losing wild free-flowing streams. The added benefits to boat fishermen could not be so conveniently substituted for the lost stream-fishing opportunities.

Fisheries experts feared not just the loss of the ten miles of trout stream buried beneath the new reservoir but damage to all fifty-one miles from Divide to the river's mouth. High water, they pointed out, would prevent fishermen from getting to the river below the dam in the good, spring fishing season when runoff would also be high. Upstream the river would receive a new planting of carp each year from the rough fish production in the warmer reservoir waters. Montana fisheries specialists, drawing on their experience with other reservoirs, concluded that on such projects trout streams are "invariably damaged." As evidence they pointed to the nearby Beaverhead, another trout stream known nationally among fishermen. Since Canyon Ferry Dam was installed on that stream, the first mile and three-quarters of the river below the dam has suffered severe fish kills at least twice, as decaying vegetation fed lethal hydrogen sulphide into the water. Still another pollutant common to irrigation systems is silt carried from the watered fields back into the main streams.

As a matter of adding machine calculations, the cost of such projects is split into subtotals, reimbursable, and non-reimbursable. Non-reimbursable on the Jefferson-Whitehall project was $14 million, supposedly marked for expenditure by taxpayers in the national good. But before we relax in the belief that the remaining $63½ million will eventually be returned to the taxpayers, we should, as practiced shoppers anywhere do, take a closer look at what we buy. To begin, the Bureau of Reclamation figures the $63½ million should be paid back within one hundred years. Of the total, during that time, the irrigators using the water will pay $8,004,250.

Still to be scraped up from some source is about $55 million. The Bureau of Reclamation proposes to employ here its basin technique, permitting it to make payments on one project with income from another. Once they dam the Big Hole River, they can pay the remainder of the cost from sales of electric power generated downstream at dams in the Missouri River Basin. This prospect might look brighter except for the poor profit rating of the power producing facilities in the Missouri River Basin. An audit dated April, 1962, was said to be the most recent accounting available of the profit-and-loss picture for Missouri River Basin power. Covering fiscal year 1959-60, this document revealed that after paying other current operating expenses, the power revenues fell $1,912,000 short of even paying interest due on the Missouri River Basin power projects themselves.

This is the source from which the Bureau anticipates $55 million profits. Privately operated, it might well be bankrupt.

There still remains to be answered perhaps the most basic of all questions in this controversy, whether or not the Bureau of Reclamation or any other building agency should be permitted to make final decisions on whether or not a project is too costly. Reclamation can be forgiven for searching around for the lowest cost plan. It found one such spot in the Big Hole. Small dam, big lake. As engineers they are on solid ground. But they have not satisfactorily answered the question as to whether or not the valley might be a better national resource left in its original form.

Arizona is perhaps an extreme example of a state that has mined its water resources and come face to face with the spectre of running out of reserves. Especially since World War II, Arizona has been using her limited water resources at a grand rate. She turned to pumping from her underground supplies and mined these sources so diligently they began drying up, and thousands of once-watered acres have been turned back to the desert. Under these pressures, and with most of the good dam sites already used up, the Bureau of Reclamation saw the opportunity to set in motion a gigantic project it had long considered, the damming of the mighty Colorado River in the heart of the Grand Canyon, not with one but with two tremendous concrete dams.

Born of ice waters from the melting snow pack along the continental divide in Wyoming and in Colorado's Rocky Mountain National Park, the Colorado flows on for 1400 miles toward the Gulf of California. En route it gathers water from thousands of tributary creeks, and from such rivers as the Green, San Juan, and the Virgin. Without this great river much of the

land in the seven states it touches would be unin-
habitable for humans. Even with it, there is never
enough water to satisfy all the needs.

About halfway along its route to the sea, the
Colorado begins a 280-mile rush through the Grand
Canyon. Erosion is the craftsman here, and water,
wind, frost, and time its tools. The Grand Canyon
is still growing. It is a mile deep and averages about
eight miles wide from rim to rim. It could, at least
in theory, become in some future age hundreds of
feet deeper than it is, if left unmolested. Over eons
of time, as the river cut its path through the rock
layes, the earth rose. This additional elevation lent
speed to the flowing water. As a result, the Colorado
has cut its course into the heart of the earth, down
to the oldest layers of rock known to geologists. Visitors, seeking the real story which the Grand Canyon
has to tell, may take the trip along the twisting narrow trails to the riverbed on the canyon floor. There
are two ways to get down into the bottom of the
canyon, one by foot, the other by mule. Cut off from
the world outside, the Havasupai Indians occupy their
tiny reservation on the floor of the canyon.

The ribbonlike trail winds its way downward along
the canyon walls which depict the geologic ages of
the earth. First, nearest the rim and supporting the
vegetation on top, is the Kaibab limestone, eight
hundred feet thick. Then there is a three hundred-foot
gray layer of Coconino sandstone. Next come the
varied colors of the Supai formation, a series of red
sandstones and shales eleven hundred feet thick. Below this, for five hundred feet, is the Redwall limestone, which is gray as rocks first break from it, but
over the years gathers its red stain from waters washing down over the red rocks above. Near the bottom
of the canyon is a greenish shale, eight hundred feet
thick—the Tonto group. It rests on a sandstone bed

150 feet thick at the canyon's bottom. Beneath this layer of sandstone, and exposed in places, is the granite crust which was the surface of the earth when the planet formed and cooled; it is the oldest of known rock formations.

Through this canyon flows the Colorado, falling about twelve feet to the mile, averaging three hundred feet wide, thirty feet deep, and always muddy with the silt from its watershed. Since the earliest days of the white man's coming to the continent this canyon has stirred the imagination of explorers. In one of the greatest adventure stories of history, Major John Wesley Powell, one-armed veteran of the Civil War, became, in 1869, the first man to explore the length of the Grand Canyon and live to write about it. He started with four boats and nine men and fought the white water cataracts for three months. He came out downriver a thousand miles, minus two boats and four men. Today, in safer equipment, about 6000 adventuresome vacationers and sportsmen a year still make white water runs here.

Advocates of dams within the Grand Canyon anticipated from the beginning that they would encounter resistance, but the Bureau of Reclamation within the Department of the Interior calculated that it could deal with opposition as it had in the past. There would be the Sierra Club, Wilderness Society, and a handful of others that the dam builders know as the "preservationists"—all in all, nothing to worry about.

Floyd E. Dominy, Commissioner of the Bureau of Reclamation, had constructed a large, carefully built model of the canyon and its dams. This he displayed to Secretary of the Interior Stewart L. Udall, to demonstrate that the planned "improvements" would not detract from the Grand Canyon scenery.

Meanwhile, the bill which would have authorized

these structures was made ready and introduced by
Morris Udall, Representative to Congress from Arizona. The bill called for two dams within the Grand
Canyon. The National Park extends along the river
for one hundred and five miles. Grand Canyon National Monument connects with it downstream. What
the reclamation forces planned was to build one dam
at Bridge Canyon below the National Monument and
a second one at Marble Canyon above the National
Park. Bridge Canyon Dam would back water through
the monument and thirteen miles into the park. To
make certain the Indian tribe at the bottom of Grand
Canyon would support the move, the reclamation
forces promised increased tourist trade from motor-
boaters and picnickers, and the benefits coming from
the anticipated influx of federal dollars to the riverbed. They had also changed the name of this dam
from Bridge Canyon to Hualapai. It should be pointed
out here that both Stewart Udall and his brother
Morris had long records of conscientious effort and
accomplishment as conservationists and that the water
needs of the Southwest are real and critical. The
waters of the Colorado have long been among the
most coveted in the world. The states touched by the
river want, and need, these waters each for itself.
Mexico, with which the United States shares the river,
comes in for its share in keeping with a treaty signed
in 1944.

As finally introduced, the bill that would have
authorized the dams within the canyon, promised
many things to many westerners whose support was
needed if the bill was to pass. There was one item
of $360 million for reclamation projects upstream in
Utah, Colorado, and Wyoming. Three of these projects
lay within the district of Representative Wayne Aspi-
nall, of Colorado, Chairman of the House Interior
Committee. Sections of Texas and Kansas—which are

outside the Colorado River watershed—were gathered into the fold with promises written into the bill to grant projects in those states. When finally ready for consideration, the bill had fattened to become a $1.7 billion package.

Before the hearings were long underway, testimony revealed that, like an iceberg, the largest part of the plan was still hidden from public view. The plan, so far known as CAP or the Central Arizona Project, was the part above the surface.

Largely for the benefit of California, and especially Los Angeles, the final element in the bill was to create a National Water Commission. This group would be directed to begin studying the possibilities of feeding waters from other sources into the ever-thirsty Colorado. The study, to be completed by 1969, would have been followed by the drawing up of plans for the project, which is known as the Pacific Southwest Water Plan—the underwater part of the iceberg. The total cost was to be $8 billion. The idea did not especially appeal to politicians from Washington and Oregon who were quick to realize that the scheme was to draw water eventually from the brawling Columbia, and direct it through a complicated maze of tunnels, aqueducts, and pipelines, until it emptied into the Colorado.

Previously, the seven states claiming the Colorado were also responsible for delivering to Mexico its fair portion of Colorado River waters. But the new bill would change this and shift the responsibility for supplying the Mexican quota to the federal government. To obtain this water and meet its international obligations—so the reasoning went—the government would have to tap the Columbia, thus shifting to the federal taxpayer the cost of this seven-state obligation. It was an interesting plan for tapping the federal treasury for an increasing subsidy for reclamation projects.

Strangely, the Bureau of Reclamation did not anticipate using any of the water from the Grand Canyon reservoirs for irrigation or other direct purposes. By the Bureau's own description, these dams were "cash registers." The explanation for this strange terminology was to be found once more in the procedure which enables Reclamation to build up a "basin account," then use revenues so acquired for whatever projects it deems desirable. The two dams in the Grand Canyon, instead of supplying irrigation water, would supply only electric power or money. Their sole purpose was to stack up the waters flowing down the canyon and feed them through turbines. The funds acquired this way could be used later to bring water to the arid sections of Arizona and a few other locations.

Well before the bill was to come to the floor of Congress in August, 1966, the big fight was in full flower. On one side were the "reclamation forces," strong men willing to forge ahead, firm in the belief that what the West did, even to desecrating the Grand Canyon, was the concern of only the West. On the other side were those convinced that the Grand Canyon belongs, not to any state or governmental bureau alone, but to the entire nation.

Led by the uncompromising Sierra Club, with its hard-fighting David Brower at the front, the conservation forces began lining up expert witnesses. Joining the Sierra Club was practically every national conservation organization in the country. But even more important was the swelling public opinion that began to plague the advocates of the reclamation plan. It soon became plain that Americans everywhere considered the fate of the Grand Canyon their concern.

Opposition to the dam builders centered around

two basic points. One was the question of economic feasibility. The other was precisely what effect the structures would have on the Grand Canyon. Would they indeed, as the reclamation forces insisted, have no adverse effect? Some even insisted that the reservoirs were good because vacationers could then see unknown parts of the canyon painlessly. From the venerable canyon walls would echo the joyous noises of water skiers and speedboaters. The government does not owe "millions of Americans" a painless look at any segment of the land. More than providing us a look at wilderness we have not viewed, it owes us reassurance that the last remnants of wild America will be safe from exploiters.

The anticipated life of the lakes would be one hundred years. At the end of which time we could assume that the river would have filled with silt and our multimillion-dollar "cash registers" could be discarded or replaced.

Congressmen, amazed at the outpouring of mail from constituents, began speaking up with increasing frequency against the project. On the Senate floor in June, 1966, Senator Clifford P. Case of New Jersey said, "At a time when the President is pressing a campaign to preserve natural beauty, Congress is being asked to approve a plan that would destroy a great part and radically change what remained of the Grand Canyon of the Colorado . . . The length of the Grand Canyon National Monument and thirteen miles of the national park would be flooded behind Bridge Canyon Dam. The Marble Gorge Dam would create a lake three hundred feet deep behind it and would inundate fifty miles of the upper Grand Canyon . . . I would rather pay the additional taxes . . . to fund the water-diversion project than to sell what I regard as the birthright of our people for a mess of pottage . . . As some conservationists have put it, 'a living laboratory of stream erosion would be turned into a static museum piece.'"

Representative John P. Saylor of Pennsylvania labeled the idea a "selfish scheme," and other legislators expressed themselves similarly. It still looked as if the bill might be brought to the floor of the House and passed, until the Sierra Club began, during the summer of 1966, condemning the plan in a series of full-page advertisements in the New York *Times*. In response to the claim that the reservoirs would bring tourists closer to the canyon walls, one of these messengers asked, "Should we also flood the Sistine Chapel so tourists can get nearer the ceiling?" Another, using a direct quote from one of the introduced Grand Canyon bills, was headlined "Grand Canyon National Monument Is Hereby Abolished."

The flood of mail to Washington increased. One legislator complained that the Grand Canyon was even drawing more mail than the war in Vietnam. Gradually the chances for the grand scheme in the Grand Canyon began looking slimmer. The reclamation forces were disgruntled about the whole development and quick to place blame on the doorstep of the "supposed conservationists," especially Dave Brower and the Sierra Club.

Shortly after one New York *Times* advertisement appeared, an official communiqué reached the San Francisco headquarters of the Sierra Club from the offices of the Bureau of Internal Revenue. That tax collecting agency announced it was reviewing immediately the Sierra Club's tax exempt status. The Sierra Club was later informed that contributions to it could no longer be considered as tax exempt because it was attempting to influence legislation. Resulting publicity from this singling out of the Sierra Club bought another flood of letters condemning the Grand Canyon dams. There also came a flurry of new memberships to the Sierra Club which was losing its larger contributors because of the tax ruling.

From the lengthy discussions, both in and out of congressional hearing rooms, had come evidence that the dams did not measure up economically. Among the professional people who had stepped forward volunteering their services to save the Grand Canyon were two noted economists, Dr. Alan P. Carlin and Dr. William E. Hoehn. Their calculations showed that at a realistic 5 per cent interest rate the Hualapai Dam would return not the 2.0 to 1 benefit-cost ratio the Bureau claimed, but 0.52 to 1, while the Marble Canyon Dam, instead of the claimed benefit-cost ratio of 1.7 to 1, was shown to have a potential closer to 0.79 to 1. In view of such testimony the sacrifice of the Grand Canyon looked less desirable than ever. It was already known that profit making power companies were rapidly turning for economy reasons to atomic-power plants.

The conservation forces relaxed somewhat when Secretary Udall, after a year of studying the problem from all angles, reversed his original thinking and withdrew his support. The campaign had been bitter medicine for the reclamationists long accustomed to having their way.

In the early days of the fight, when the Bureau of Reclamation first announced the plans, knowledgeable bettors would have put their money on the dam builders. The chances of stopping them, and saving the Grand Canyon from the invaders, seemed slim. But in this canyon, the American citizen should have learned a lesson, it *is* possible to stop the dam builders.

Brought out of the fog in which the Bureau of Reclamation had obscured the calculations, the real purpose of the dams had become increasingly evident. Dave Brower of the Sierra Club stated it succinctly. "The true purpose of the Grand Canyon dams," he told the country, "is to provide a respectable front for the siphoning of hundreds of millions—even billions—of dollars from the U. S. Treasury to the Basin account. Because the dams are not economically justified, the cost to the U. S. Treasury will be far greater than if direct subsidies were made . . . But all of this counts for little to the proponents of the dams, who believe that it is easier to raid the Treasury for more money, if the raid is disguised, than it is to obtain a direct . . . subsidy . . ."

If the Bureau of Reclamation's dam builders were turned back at the Grand Canyon, it was soon apparent this was viewed only as a skirmish in a continuing battle. Incredibly, the Bureau of Reclamation was already planning to invade the country's first designated wilderness area with one of its big bodies of slack water.

Lying to the north and west of Silver City, New Mexico, is a rugged land of incomparable wild mountain country with high trails, deep forests, and miles of tumbling trout waters. It was in this Gila Mountains country that the national wilderness system was born. Shortly after he went to work for the U. S. Forest Service in the southwest, the late Aldo Leopold saw in this spectacular and rugged region a segment of America that should always remain free of highways and other developments. By 1924 he had convinced others of the value of setting aside such areas. That year the U. S. Forest Service designated the Gila as the first official wilderness area. When the Wilderness Preservation Act of 1964 was passed the Gila was included. Now only a few years later, it was Reclamation's target.

There appeared within the proposed Central Arizona Project-Colorado River Bill, a vaguely described structure called the Hooker Dam. With it, Reclamation proposed to block off the free-flowing Gila River near the southern border of the famed wilderness area. The reservoir behind the dam promised mass recreation. How many miles the waters would extend into the wilderness was difficult to tell because Reclamation had not yet let the outside world in on particulars of the dam they would build there. There had been no recent study on the dam. There was no benefit-cost ratio figure to discredit it because it was lumped with other proposed structures in the Central Arizona Project. Measured on its own worth alone, it could scarcely have been approved. As reported by the Izaak Walton League and other watchful conservation groups, only 4 per cent of the annual 18,000 acre-feet of water promised New Mexico from behind Hooker would go to irrigation. Largely, the impounded water was expected to go for the use of one major industry in the area, the Phelps Dodge Corporation.

Farther down the Gila were at least two alternate sites that would have saved the Gila Wilderness Area from invasion. But to the Bureau of Reclamation this plan to invade the nation's wilderness system was viewed as a welcome test case. If Congress granted this violation of the wilderness scene, others could surely follow. The precedent would be set, the defense penetrated.

Even as it asked authorization to dam the Gila, the Bureau of Reclamation turned its beaverlike vision toward the famed Bob Marshall Wilderness, enchanted highland of northwestern Montana. In this great wild area roams our second largest herd of elk. Pack outfitters lead parties into the heart of the Bob Marshall on unforgettable fishing, camping, hunting, and exploring trips. Here the Bureau of Reclamation has been agitating to dam the Sun River, which would reduce the Bob Marshall Wilderness by perhaps 55,000 acres. The impoundment would permanently flood out seventeen miles of superb trout stream, and cut across the migration routs of the elk passing from wintering grounds in the valleys to summer range in the high meadows.

Meanwhile, another proposed dam would flood portions of the wilderness in Glacier National Park. Still other projects threaten primitive areas in Idaho, Utah's High Uintas, and the Flat Tops Wilderness in Colorado. Plainly, the Bureau of Reclamation views the nation's wilderness program as a barrier to its own expansion. We must be vigilant and vociferous in our opposition to such unnecessary works if we are to save our wilderness areas.

Seldom noted for its ability to charm its opponents, the Bureau of Reclamation had, earlier, surprised some circles when during the Grand Canyon struggle, it turned to poetry. It composed and published "Jewel of the Colorado," a beautifully illustrated booklet in full and costly color. This publication told of the wonders of Lake Powell backed up behind the Glen Canyon Dam, and in singing these praises, promised like rewards in the Grand Canyon if people would come to their senses and permit the construction there of the Hualapai and Marble Canyon dams. Finally the authors lapsed into dubious poetic rhapsody. Overprinted on a picture of blue waters backed up against a red sandstone cliff was this thought to touch the hearts of dam builders everywhere.

> "To have a deep blue lake
> Where no lake was before
> Seems to bring man
> A little closer to God."

8. The Highwaymen

It was a scorching hot day, and I was glad to escape to the air-conditioned hallways of the big government building, housing the Department of Transportation. The civil servant I sought was a salty professional public relations man in the service of the road builders. He gave me an insight into the driving force which guides the country's mammoth road building industry across the American landscape. He helped me realize that the machines that build roads are made to respond only to the engineers. The highway planners neither seek nor welcome back seat driving from the rest of the citizenry.

I mentioned a few tender places on the American map, nature preserves that conservationists had struggled to save, wildlife refuges, and public parks that had fallen beneath the concrete complex. "These do-gooders," he snapped, "bitch and complain and they don't make sense. Where would we be if it weren't for roads?"

This was supposed to answer all questions. We would, of course, be in the mud, where no one wants to be. But conservationists notice that engineers utilize such sweeping generalizations to minimize arguments of those seeking to have them occasionally change their routes or alter their plans. "How can you argue with the figures?" I was asked by the civil servant. "In the past year, use of the Interstate System has increased 8.6 times over the year before. This is almost twice the increase for the preceding year. People approve what we're doing; they approve it with their votes for extra funds."

My mind flashed back to a little river in a green valley in the heart of Ohio. The valley of the Olentangy is no Grand Canyon, or even a South Fork of the Cumberland. But it was once a pleasant place where a gentle stream flowed over a rocky creekbed, between walls of tall green trees. And in the midst of a bustling crowded world, it was a rare treasure.

Then the Ohio Department of Highways decided to build a new thruway northward out of Columbus. They chose as their route the streambed of the shallow Olentangy. It would provide for easy grading and solid foundation. There arose a great public debate along the banks of the Olentangy, between the highway planners who measure beauty in concrete terms, and the citizens who loved their green and gentle valley. The fight spread across the pages of Columbus newspapers, and public officials jumped in on the side of the highway planners—and progress.

Consequently, the riverbanks were scalped, and the trees removed. Recently I had driven down the lacerated valley. I saw an aged couple standing in their yard, watching the valley die before their eyes. Sad-eyed, they stood in hopeless resignation. Too often, this is all the average citizen can do when the highway builders come. Today a new highway stretches like an overlay map on the sacrificed valley of the Olentangy, and the river finds its way around the concrete stilts on which sections of the highway perch.

Still expressing his opinion of those who would stand in the path of progress, the highway official was saying, "I hear all this about parks. I wonder where the people are in the parks. I've been to the parks. Most of the time they're empty. If there is a park in the way of a planned highway, what's to keep us from going out in the country and making a new park where no road is planned? These goddam clowns who fight us don't seem to understand that people want roads."

His thinking typifies the highway engineer's feeling about his work—that he is in close rapport with all but a lunatic fringe, and all who disagree with him become public enemies. It is little wonder that over the years, conservationists have learned to fear for the safety of the landscape's natural features. Nobody laughs when the highway planners sit down at their drafting boards.

River valleys and mountain vistas, wildlife refuges and city parks, historic sites and deep wilderness are neither respected nor safe before them. They bridge the deepest canyons, tunnel beneath the rivers, slash away the mountainsides, and fill in the valleys if they choose. Where the highway shall go has historically been determined on the basis of cost per mile alone. Too seldom is there an effort to calculate the value of landscape features to be sacrificed. The grove of towering tulip poplars where people like to walk at their leisure, the park where children have played for generations, the little marsh harboring a unique community of plants and animals, or even a great wildlife refuge—all lack the value of a square yard of concrete.

Road builders have developed a knack for planning their routes through public lands. Here they find few buildings in their path, and few private property owners with whom they must deal and dicker. It was National Park Service Director, George B. Hartzog, Jr., who said in the White House Conference on Natural Beauty in 1965, "The problem up to this point has been this philosophy: that if it is a park, it is free, and, certainly, if it is a park, it is open. So it is easy.

"Somehow they seem to be able," added Hartzog speaking of the highway planners, "to find a blue pencil that hits the green spot."

Characteristically, the planners offer no alternate

routes, though alternates exist. Too often the public has been appraised of the selected routes as if blind approval is expected. But in Columbus, Ohio, an editorial writer for the *Citizen Journal*, speaking of the assault on the Olentangy, drew attention to a basic weakness in our highway planning. "Civil engineers are expert road-construction planners," he said, "but they are not community planners. This freeway should be part of a broad community plan. It should include the saving of natural beauty as well as the building of a road."

In 1960, Montana sent the ex-associate justice of its Supreme Court, Lee Metcalf, a determined fighter in the ranks of the conservationists, to the United States Senate. Senator Metcalf rapidly became known as a leading advocate of better planning in our national highway program. "Soon after ground was broken on this expanded program," he said, speaking of the 41,000-mile national Interstate System, "we began to realize that those farsighted conservationists of the past who had laid out what was to become a nationwide network of recreation lands, were in reality the master highway planners of all time. This was documented by reports from throughout the nation that present day highway planners were indeed building on the past—through one recreation area and on to the next."

Writing in the Sierra Club Bulletin in January, 1964, Senator Metcalf added, "Direct damage resulted from building highways in streambeds and from removing— for fill and for use in making concrete—the streambed gravel that is so vital to fish spawning and fish food production. Meandering streams, lined with erosion-controlling vegetation, were bulldozed into sterile shoots, alternately scoured and silted, always ruined."

Losses at the hands of highway planners are widespread. To Senator Metcalf came a report from his own state of a highway routed into a trout stream to avoid the cost of moving a power line. Meanwhile in Utah, highway planners opposed redesigning part of a highway to save a portion of the Logan River. Biologists in South Dakota sadly reported that in the famed Black Hills region of their state, no more than 160 miles of streams suitable for trout remained. Once there had been 1200 miles. What had happened to South Dakota's trout streams? Largely they had been sacrificed to highways or lost to the sediment that washes into them from highway construction.

Near Salamanca, New York, the Seneca Indians have a reservation. Since George Washington's treaty with them in 1794, they have held this land. Following an ancient Indian trail down the valley and through the reservation, was a two-lane highway. The State Department of Transportation decided to replace it with a four-lane freeway. The tribe had already lost a bout with the Corps of Engineers which built the Kinzua Dam, flooding one third of their land. The highway would slice through the middle of their remaining holdings. They went to court. They lost. The Senecas saw the remainder of their land bisected by a four-lane, fenced-in superhighway.

In northern Alabama, on the TVA Wheeler Reservoir, the U. S. Fish and Wildlife Service established the 35,000-acre Wheeler National Wildlife Refuge. It is considered a vital link in the Atlantic Flyway and particularly important in the efforts to extend the Canada goose flocks southward once more. Although the sloughs and wet fields along the banks of the Tennessee River do not lie in the traditional Canada Goose Flyway, the waterfowl managers have met outstanding success in their efforts to encourage the geese to use this major stop in a series of resting and feeding areas which would guide them ultimately into Florida. So successful had the goose management program on the refuge been that biologists succeeded in building the flocks up to peaks of 85,000 during fall migration periods. But the Alabama highway department decided that Interstate 65 should cross the Wheeler Refuge. Wildlife biologists, aware of the fact that geese possess an inherent dread of elevated structures, feared for what the proposed superhighway, on its stilts, would do to their prospering goose flock.

When he first heard of this proposal, Secretary of the Interior Stewart L. Udall announced that the highway planners would be denied a right-of-way through Wheeler Refuge. But the highwaymen had the muscle. Eventually the Secretary withdrew his objections. The highwaymen had won again.

In Key West, Florida, the fathers of that vacation city in the sun would like a new highway connecting them with the mainland—this one, it has been suggested, could pass through the unique Everglades National Park. And in Georgia, highway engineers once considered routing a highway through the wild beauty of Okefenokee National Wildlife Refuge.

Towering hundreds of feet over the valley of the Pemigewasset River in New Hampshire a series of ledges form the famous Great Stone Face. This is the heart of the cherished White Mountain vacation area, especially popular when autumn splashes brilliant colors up the mountainside and across the hardwood forest. It has been called New Hampshire's greatest natural asset. A modest highway, twisting and turning along the river valley, had long carried leisurely traffic into this recreational area. The state once determined that fewer than 20 per cent of the travelers coming to Franconia Notch are interested in going to points beyond. But instead of routing the planned Interstate 93 around the area, thus avoiding any potential damage to a scenic wonder, New Hampshire's highway engineers decided that it would penetrate Franconia

Notch. In view of the fact that many of the visitors are from out of state, and that 90 per cent of the funds to build the highway come from the federal government, such decisions logically should rest with an agency other than the State Highway Department.

Highway planners in California, seeking ways to improve Route 40, eliminated almost a mile of the fishing waters of the south fork of the Yuba River. The method was simple—the same as that along the Olentangy—they proclaimed the streambed a roadbed and relocated and straightened the Yuba.

Far to the east, an Interstate was being routed through the heart of Memphis, slashing across that city's old and cherished wildlife refuge and natural area, Overton Park. Angry Memphis citizens fought a valiant rearguard action to save Overton Park from the approaching bulldozers, but the city fathers, who thought that this route would bring added traffic to the downtown business section, had political power enough to ignore Overton Park.

There are examples in every state. Highway planners have sought to build high-speed roads through California's Prairie Creek Redwood State Park. They also planned their roads up the valley of the Beaver Kill, perhaps New York's most famous trout stream. It is not so much the loss of a single natural area that is frightening. It is the sheer magnitude of the highway builders' empire—the fact that it reaches into every corner of the land. It is a great sprawling organism drawing its power from the state capitals, all loosely watched over from the control tower in Washington where, at least for federal roads, the Department of Transport dispenses funds, standardizes, and approves.

There is no question that we need highways—and good ones. In today's society and economy we need the mobility that our evolving technology has promised us. We need the superhighways. But we permit the highway planners the luxury of a final word on where a new road will go, and, in effect, what it will destroy.

This is the biggest business in America. One of every seven Americans, and one of every half-dozen businesses, is somehow connected with the empire of highway transportation.

Urging the highway builders on and helping them tell their message and defend themselves against all criticism are the satellite industries. Glance down a list of the suppliers dependent upon our continued construction of new roads. In the U. S. Department of Transportation's "Highway Statistics of 1966" there is a listing of the average materials needed for each million dollars worth of federal highway construction during the mid-1960s. Out of each million dollars (which may build less than a mile of highway) comes the payment for 62,000 board feet of lumber, 128,000 gallons of petroleum products, 31,000 pounds of explosives, 411 tons of concrete pipe, 15,000 barrels of cement, 939 tons of bituminous materials, $8600 worth of lighting, $8200 worth of signs, 3500 feet of guardrail, 9800 feet of fencing, and 80,000 man-hours of labor.

There are, in addition, the uncounted firms manufacturing drills, scrapers, earth movers, bulldozers, trucks, surveying equipment, and all the other sophisticated mechanical devices which contribute to the construction of a modern highway.

The halls of Congress are populated by powerful, skilled, determined lobbyists pleading the cause of the highway industry and those who supply it. For 1968, the federal government distributed $4,352,000,000 to the states for highway programs. And the highway lobbyists are at work, not only in the federal capitol but in statehouses across the nation.

Since 1902 the American Road Builders Association has coordinated the efforts and resources of all those holding economic interests in the ever-growing highway complex. The Association stands ready and willing. "At the invitation or request of Congressional committees, ARBA compiles information," it says, "pertaining to the need for and benefits of highways . . . and presents this information to Congress in the form of testimony on highway and airport bills." Out of the Washington offices of ARBA comes a steady flow of newspaper releases, "speeches of the month" for delivery to local fraternal groups, and other propaganda promoting the aims of the road builders. Among ARBA membes 40 per cent are highway contractors, 40 per cent highway engineers and officials from across the country, and 20 per cent are listed by ARBA as "manufacturers, distributors, producers and suppliers of materials and services, consulting engineers, bankers, educators and engineering students and members of state good-road associations."

The State Highway Directors, but more realistically their district engineers, are the men responsible for selecting the routes which our highways follow. Such choices are subject to approval by the U. S. Bureau of Public Roads. But it is the state worker, too often subjected to local pressures by Main Street businesses, who shoulders the real responsibility. "In the use of federal aid for highway construction," says the U. S. Department of Transportation, *Highway Statistics 1966*, "the states determine the system to be improved, the projects to be built, and the design and construction standards to be used. They make the surveys and plans, let the contracts, and supervise the construction. In all of these steps the states consult with and obtain the approval of the Bureau of Public Roads, acting for the federal government. The roads remain under the administrative control of the states, who are responsible for their operation and maintenance."

To the road builders, and generally speaking for the rest of us too, top priority goes to the vast system of interstate highways with which we are connecting all parts of the country. Beginning with the Federal Highway Act of 1944, the job was finally scheduled for completion in 1972, at an estimated $56.5 billion for 41,000 miles. With 90 per cent paid by federal funds, these roads have an average cost in rural areas of $732,000 per mile, and in urban areas a per-mile cost of $3,739,000. The concrete for them alone, we are told, would build six sidewalks to the moon, a statistic which may provide imaginative planners with something to think about. A modern interstate highway through a rural area calls for nine times as much excavation as our major roads of a generation ago.

In recent times there has been a growing concern over the failure of highway planners to make serious effort to fit their works to the nature of the land. "Our highways must be in harmony with the communities and countrysides of which they are part," President Johnson told the Congress in March of 1968. "Too often in the past, this need has received little more than lip service."

Congress in 1966 reached a milestone with passage of the Department of Transportation Act. The heart of that act, to conservationists worried about the destructive activities of the highway builders, was Section 4 (f). This section forbade the Secretary of Transportation from approving the use of any highway projects using federal money to build a road through public parks, recreation areas, wildlife refuges, and historic sites, ". . . unless there is no feasible and prudent alternative." But highway builders fretted under this restriction. They sought a way to have it removed. They found it in 1968. Only two years after Congress had told them to keep their bulldozers out of parks and refuges, the Federal-Aid Highway Act of 1968 so weakened the language of the controversial Section 4 (f) that as the National Wildlife Federation said, it ". . . would scuttle protection in the Department of Transportation Act for parks, wildlife refuges, recreation areas, and historic sites." The House of Representatives Committee on Public Works freed the highway engineers of the two-year restriction against invading valued public lands by rewording the law so the Secretary of Transportation, instead of being barred from approving use of federal funds for such purposes, was now required only to give "consideration" to alternatives. As the Citizens Committee on Natural Resources was quick to point out, ". . . highway planners can readily consider and reject. . . ." In spite of the efforts of conservation organizations the law was forced through. Said the Citizens Committee on Natural Resources, "No park, monument, wildlife or waterfowl refuge, public-recreation area or historic site in America will be safe from assault by highway builders."

Passage of the law unleashed the bulldozers. The newly written legislation also extended the interstate highway system by 1500 miles without any serious study of where and how much, if at all, the Interstate System should be enlarged. Congress had, in addition, taken away funds for highway beautification and succeeded in deleting those portions of former legislation aimed at removing offensive billboards from along America's highways. Even Secretary of Transportation Alan S. Boyd had asked that the sections of the old law dealing with highway beautification and the protection of valued publicly owned areas be left unchanged. But the highway builders, seeking freedom from all restrictions, won out.

What were leaders of the highway industry thinking, as the 41,000-mile Interstate System neared com-

Kentucky's Cumberland Falls, with a drop of 68 feet, is one of the largest in North America and the home of the only moon-bow in the Western Hemisphere. The Corps of Engineers had a plan to turn the Falls on and off like a faucet without, they were confident, impairing the Falls's "scenic effectiveness." *Photo by Tourist and Travel Commission, Frankfort, Kentucky.*

Progress in the form of a Corps of Engineers dam now completed elsewhere on the Cumberland River in Kentucky.

The inexorable spread of housing developments such as this one in the Ohio River bottom creates the demand for flood-control dams. The question is: do they really solve the problem?

According to an anonymous poet, the Bureau of Reclamation's Glen Canyon Dam at Page, Arizona, brought yachtsmen and water skiers on the newly created Lake Powell about ninety feet closer to God.

The creators of scenes like this typical highway maze are unlikely to show much understanding of landscape and wildlife, much less human ecology.

Shell dredging San Antonio Bay in Texas has provided the whooping cranes, whose tenuous existence is carried on in wintering grounds nearby, with a new and menacing neighbor.

The stripped corpse of a mountain in Kentucky.

Looming high over a small shack and a trailer is the latest in strip-mining efficiency. *Photo by Karl H. Maslowski.*

Earmarked for draining by the Corps of Engineers, this little remnant cypress swamp in western Kentucky was purchased by the Nature Conservancy and saved. How many such places throughout the land will not be rescued by a similar buyer? *Photo by Karl H. Maslowski.*

pletion? For years this giant project—the biggest civil work project in the history of the world—had kept the planners busy and the machinery moving. What would happen to all this vast mechanism when the last mile of the Interstate System lay bright and new upon the landscape? It would be naïve to think that the highway planners would consider their work completed.

One day in Washington I asked an official in the Department of Transport, "When do you think you will complete the Interstate System?"

For a moment he looked at me with a quizzical smile and then said, "Do you think it *will* be completed?" He knew that already the U. S. Department of Transportation had conducted a state-by-state survey, not to learn when the Interstate Highway System would be completed, but to ask how much additional mileage each state highway director thought his state might need after the 41,000 miles was finished. Shortly the answers were in and totaled. The State Highway Directors felt the 41,000 miles originally established by law was less than one-half what they really needed. Together, they foresaw the need for 50,000 miles or about 125 per cent more than the original plan had called for—only twelve years earlier.

Where will these roads be built? Of the interstate highways in the original plan at least one-third stretched across new rights-of-way. And a mile of such superhighway took nine times as much acreage as a mile of a major road a generation earlier.

Another recently devised possibility for keeping America's road builders busier than ever appeared in June, 1966. The Government Printing Office published a 254-page book called *Proposed Program for Scenic Roads and Parkways*. The ideas incorporated in this volume had come from many branches of government, ranging from the Department of Defense to the National Park Service. But the writing of the report, as I was assured in Washington, was handled by the road builders—the U. S. Department of Transport. An official of that department told me frankly, "We wrote the report. But I was against it, because I don't think people will use the scenic roads."

This plan for a network of national scenic roads worried conservationists from the beginning. It apparently originated as a result of the finding by the new Bureau of Outdoor Recreation within the Department of the Interior, that "Driving for pleasure is America's chief outdoor recreation."

This finding attracted presidential attention. A 1962 Executive Order grouped the secretaries of Interior, Agriculture, Defense, Commerce, and Health, Education and Welfare, along with the Administrator of the Housing and Home Finance Agency, and Chairman of the Tennessee Valley Authority into the President's Recreation Advisory Council. By April, 1964, the council had advocated that ". . . a national program of scenic roads and parkways be developed." As far as the council was concerned, even then, there seemed to be no further question about the real need for a national system of scenic roads to lead auto-borne adventurers into the wilderness.

All state and federal agencies were requested to turn in their suggestions for scenic highways and parkways. When all the nominations were in, and the figures totaled, the nation could boast 136,500 miles which state officials considered worthy of such designation. Some of this was existing highway that would be redesignated and then improved to scenic highway standards. But one-third of the total was to be new roads. The anticipated cost came to $18.7 billion. The council boiled this down to a "recommended minimum program," for scenic roads to be built in one decade at a cost of about $4 billion.

Although there is doubtless some good to be found in the proposals of this study, the idea itself is enough to leave conservationists quaking. Under the cloak of a national system of highways designed to lead us into the beauty spots of the earth, what treasured wilderness would be safe? Such a program, once begun, is difficult to terminate, or even slow down. It could provide one more key to opening the remaining wilderness areas. And highways are the enemies of wilderness.

Conceivably, the driving adventurer in his upholstered chair could find his reward and stimulation if the scenic highway leads him only to naturally attractive areas which are already developed. But there is no reason to believe that the remaining wild areas would escape the attention of those piloting the program. The first report estimated that 25 per cent of the new highways would penetrate mountainous areas. There is no reason to believe that the automobile industry, and the highway construction agencies, with their dependent contractors and their scurrying lobbyists, would lead us away from the parks and refuges or agree that such areas should be safe from destruction.

The selection of routes for scenic highways rested largely on the judgment of the state highway departments. And state highway departments, with few exceptions, have shown brutal attitudes toward parks, refuges, and historic treasures.

As for paying for the proposed scenic highways, the council advanced several suggestions ranging from added taxes on gasoline to an additional excise tax on automobiles. It was noted that, once the interstate system is completed, it would take but a fraction of that money to fund the scenic roads. But many highway planners would prefer that both programs march ahead side-by-side.

Here and there the highway picture has its bright spots. Montana passed a law requiring highway builders to replace "mile for mile" any streams they destroy. Under this legislation they do not have to keep the roads out of the rivers, but no longer can the rivers end up shorter than they were before the road came. The state of New York passed legislation calling for its highway department to co-ordinate its planning and its works with its conservation department. The President's Citizens Advisory Committee on recreation and natural beauty came forward with a recommendation that the Secretary of Transportation set up a review board to deal with route selection and disputes about rights-of-way. The same committee reminded the public that "highways have an effect that reaches far beyond those who drive on them; yet our present devices for choosing locations are still based largely on requirements of the highway user rather than the community at large." The country's chief road builder, the Secretary of Transportation, told a meeting of the Migratory Bird Conservation Commission in Washington, D.C., during the Johnson Administration, that "The time is no longer with us when we can move ahead in locating transportation facilities and designing them without being concerned with and aware of the impact on the environment . . . we have not done well enough and must do better."

On this, there is wide agreement.

PART II

"The wicked flee where no man pursueth, but they make better time when someone is after them."

Charles H. Parkhurst

9. Come, Let Us Recalculate Together

There should be nothing mysterious about the yard-stick with which government construction agencies measure the worth of their projects. It is known as the benefit-cost ratio. But unlike most rulers on which the units of measurement are constant, the benefit-cost ratio has elastic tendencies. Both benefits and costs of public works projects seem to be either stretchable or shrinkable; they can be adjusted to the desires of those who do the measuring.

On the surface, the benefit-cost ratio is the same principle of economics any businessman applies to major purchases. A dairy farmer buying a cow expects her calves and milk to bring him benefits in excess of her cost. A contractor buying a new truck feels certain it will pay its way. A manufacturer installing a new die press wants its cost returned along with a margin of profit. But as a nation, we frequently embark on multimillion-dollar construction projects which are born losers. As long as the benefit-cost ratio promises a dollar back to somebody for every public dollar spent, the project may be labeled active and the concrete mixers are readied.

Questions about the relationship between benefits and cost go back at least to 1820 in the Corps of Engineers. That year the Corps was embarking on navigation improvements in Albemarle Sound, North Carolina and Congress asked for reassurance that the project was economically justified. By 1902 the new Rivers and Harbors Act was instructing the Corps to weigh benefits and costs of all their proposed projects and report on their findings. In 1936 the Flood Control Act directed that flood-control projects might be approved only if the benefits, ". . . to whomsoever they may accrue, . . ." be in excess of the estimated costs. Such wording, of course, was an open invitation to search for beneficiaries.

Today the benefit-cost ratio is the foundation of every major project whether constructed by the Corps, or the highway engineers, or the Bureau of Reclamation. Figuring possible costs and benefits of a proposed reservoir or other structure gets underway when Congress gives the word. Within the Corps of Engineers the figures are carefully reviewed by the Corps' own review board, the Board of Engineers for Rivers and Harbors. This study group consists of seven military engineers, usually generals, plus a staff of ten times as many civilian specialists. The corps points out that more than half of the projects it reviews fail to measure up. A negative finding can be disastrous to the project. The Congressman pushing for the program can either forget the requested dam as quietly as possible, or continue to bring it up periodically as long as the voters return him to Washington. Congress has been known to send the Corps back to recalculate until it dutifully brings in a set of homework figures that are not tainted with red ink.

This has been rendered increasingly possible on doubtful projects in recent times by congressional action adding new benefits which the Corps and the Bureau of Reclamation must consider in their calculations. Once concerned only with navigation, then flood control, the Corps may now assign dollar values to a lengthy list of benefits.

Meanwhile, if such "benefits" fail to bring the total high enough to cover costs, the cost figures can be reduced in various ways to make them look more respectable. Economists in recent times have, with increasing frequency, given critical study to these techniques on which we base our decisions for spending millions of dollars of the national treasury. They have made it clear that some of the most costly projects are a transparent waste of money—and river valleys. This happened to the Cross-Florida Barge Canal. The feasibility of that scheme was attacked by two economists working individually.

Writing in *Business and Economic Dimensions,* journal of the graduate faculty of the University of Florida's College of Business Administration in 1965, economist F. W. Hodge, Colonel, U. S. Army retired, summed up his findings in plain talk. "What was a laudable dream having economic merit a century ago (and dreams are notoriously persistent), now has the aspects of an economic nightmare. The probabilities are all too obvious that the ultimate cost of the Cross-Florida Barge Canal will far exceed its estimated cost."

Several years earlier, economist Charles A. Welsh, Director of the Graduate Program in Business Administration, Rollins College, Winter Park, Florida, published an incisive report on *The Economic Prospects of Cross-Florida Barge Canal Project.* "In the area of canals and waterways particularly," he wrote, "there is an urgent need to clear away the fallacies, the out-worn, indefensible illusions of general benefit or economy so often invoked to lend an aura of public interest to proposals which are in fact economically insupportable."

As for the Cross-Florida Barge Canal, according to the Welsh study, the justifications advanced are ". . . shown to rest on vulnerable assumptions of economy, inadequate investigation of economic effects, and unrealistic appraisal of benefits and costs." As the Corps returned once more to seek justification for the canal which had failed for a century to pass its economics test, it had some newly recognized "benefits" available to toss into the stew. Included was pleasure boating, $127,000 annually, a figure later reduced to $118,000. When it recalculated the case of the canal in 1958 the Corps managed to come up with a benefit-cost ratio of 1.05 to 1. Over a fifty-year period it would return a nickel profit (to someone) for every dollar invested. Obviously this would be no bargain. But the Corps' recommendation was that the project be moved onto the "active" list. The figures, however, still looked so marginal that they needed some additional shoring up. The Corps recalculated again in 1962.

The two sets of figures appeared in a June, 1962, report, "Cross-Florida Barge Canal—Chief of Engineers' Evaluation," from headquarters Department of the Army, Washington, D.C.

Annual Benefits, Annual Charges, and Benefit-Cost Ratio. A summary of the annual benefits, annual charges, and benefit-cost ratio developed for the Cross-Florida Barge Canal in the Chief of Engineers' evaluation is presented in the following tabulation. For purposes of comparison similar data for the Corps of Engineers' 1958 report are also presented.

Item	1958 Report	Present Study
Annual Benefits:		
Navigation		
Transporation savings	$7,407,000	$7,016,000
Commercial-fishing benefits	49,000	70,000
Benefits to contractors floating plant	20,000	30,000
Benefits to new-vessel deliveries	155,000	115,000
Benefits to recreational boating	127,000	118,000
Subtotal nav. benefits	$7,758,000	$7,349,000
Collateral		
Flood-control benefits	—	$ 257,000
Land-enhancement benefits	—	650,000

Subtotal, collateral benefits	—	$ 907,000
Total annual benefits	$7,758,000	$8,256,000
Total annual charges	$7,365,000	$7,039,000
Benefit-cost ratio	1.05	1.17

Office, Chief of Engineers
June 1962

Included in the new study were two figures that had not appeared in the 1958 calculations; flood-control benefits $257,000, and land-enhancement benefits $650,000, for a total of $907,000 in additional annual benefits. These, plus a few lesser changes, resulted in a benefit-cost ratio which was a somewhat more respectable 1.17 to 1. But both of those added majors benefits deserve a closer look.

The $650,000, says the Corps, will come from improved real estate values around its reservoirs built to supply the canal with water. These benefits, if they occur, will come largely to Florida real estate developers at federal expense.

The claimed flood-control credit is the result of rather strange logic. The Corps says the project will make some lands along the canal more valuable. It will then protect this valuable land from floods. So, credit the Cross-Florida Barge Canal with another $257,000 in annual benefits rendered.

It is interesting to see what would happen to the benefit-cost ratio figures if these two doubtful justifications were not figured in. Subtracting their total of $907,000 leaves an annual charge against the project of $7,349,000. Meanwhile, the Corps' calculations tell us that, in the four years between their studies, the annual charges against the project went, not up with the economic trend, but down. This is good because if the 1962 benefits were compared with the 1958 costs the Cross-Florida Barge Canal would show a $16,000 annual loss, obviously a benefit-cost ratio of less than

1 to 1. Viewed in another way, these newly claimed benefits from property enhancement and flood control, tipped the scales on a boondoggle that would ultimately cost the American people $159,900,000, plus whatever amount time and rising costs add to this Corps figure.

Then there is the matter of interest rates. The Corps used a figure of 2.5 per cent which even then, was well below the 3.5 interest rate on government bonds. And, considering the risky nature of the investment, it would seem to economists that the interest rates should be higher, not lower, than the going rate on government bonds. In 1958 if the interest had been computed at a rate one-half of one per cent higher, the benefit-cost ratio would come out less than 1 to 1.

Whatever the final cost of the Cross-Florida Barge Canal, and it will certainly be in excess of the Corps' estimates, it will be in real dollar expenditures for the taxpayer. Welsh touched on this in his conclusions, ". . . it should be clearly understood," he said, "that although the costs represent actual outlays of public funds derived from tax monies, the benefits are based on estimated savings and upon imputed or alleged economies, *not upon actual receipts of money. No revenues are received and no dividends are paid.*"

To Colonel Hodge, also, there was only one logical finding. "It can only be concluded," he wrote, "that the continuation of this project is a distinct disservice, first to the state of Florida and its citizens, and secondly, to the taxpayers of the entire United States."

Today, to arrive at the starting line on such a project, the standard procedure is to "justify" damming one more valley by claiming a lengthy list of benefits that may include flood control, water supply, fish and wildlife enhancement, recreation, water quality, power production, transportation, irrigation and land stabilization, plus general economic development. Superficially, each of these may seem to have its merits, and at times each of them does. But there is no individual item on the list, including flood control that most powerful of public appeals, that stands up under close study time after time. Even navigation, the earliest civil assignment of the Corps, has gray areas where the citizen taxpayer is justified in asking penetrating questions about canal and river projects. It is not enough to speak of "benefits" to come from a proposed canal without identifying the beneficiaries. We already know who is paying for it. Because the cost is charged against the national treasury, the benefits, as economists have often stated, should come to the nation as a whole. The consumer paying for a new canal, or river channel improvement, might properly anticipate that it will bring him lower consumer prices. But will the price of gasoline drop a penny a gallon, fertilizer sell for ten cents less per bag, or automobiles be reduced fifty dollars each because of the new Corps project?

True, the presence of a new canal might conceivably lower production costs. But are these benefits passed on to those who are taxed to pay out millions for the canal?

Instead, the benefits go more often to subsidize a select few major industries, especially river-barge companies. According to the Corps, 81 per cent of the calculated savings anticipated from the Cross-Florida Barge Canal will come to a few large industrial shippers.

The obvious question in the face of these facts is why then should not those who benefit pay for using the canal? Instead they use the public waterways free of charge. Competing forms of transportation are not so richly endowed by subsidies. Trucking firms are fond of painting on the rear of their highway giants for all to see, "This vehicle pays $4132 in taxes every year." Railroads maintain their own rights-of-way and pay real estate taxes to local governments while competing with subsidized river-barge companies.

THE FLOOD CONTROL MYTH

Of all the arguments the dam builders muster to favor their reservoirs, the prevention of floods carries the greatest promise of widespread public support. A bad flood can do the Corps of Engineers a world of good. In June, 1936, Congress, reacting to damaging floods in the valley of the Mississippi and its tributaries, passed a flood control act. Dams and levees erected as a result through the following three decades cost Americans more than $7 billion. One might assume this brought a gradual lowering of losses to flood waters. But the assumption would be unjustified. When the flood control act was passed, our annual losses to floods were computed at $250 million. Three decades later, with the new flood control structures, the losses had risen to $965 million.

Floods are natural phenomena. High waters came to the river valleys in prehistoric times. The earliest travelers recorded accounts of floods. Rivers have always used their flood plains from time to time, as rising waters escaped their banks. The trouble is that men have insisted on invading these flood plains. But why have the very structures built to diminish flood damage, increased it instead? The answer is simple enough; the new dams, promising to reduce the severity of floods, encourage developers to build in the flood plains downstream.

The public often places more faith in the ability of a dam to hold back flood waters than the Corps itself does. The Corps does not attempt to design dams that will eliminate all floods. Such structures would ordinarily be too costly to qualify no matter how the figures were juggled. Each project has a flood level for which it is designed—the "project flood." Bigger floods—whether they come once in a decade or once in a century—escape the riverbanks and spread across the flood plains where developers have erected high-value structures.

Those of us who invest in flood control dams, and all of us do, should understand that the usefulness of these reservoirs diminishes as they age. As the reservoir fills with sediment, it can store less water. At the same time the growing population puts added demands on water resources. The only solution seems to be to build additional reservoirs which will, in turn, fill with sediment. Every reservoir has a life expectancy although the scientists cannot always agree on what it is. When Hoover Dam was completed in 1936, Lake Mead's storage capacity was 32,471,000 acre-feet. Three decades later sediment had reduced the capacity by more than 15 per cent to 27,377,000 acre-feet. The rate of sedimentation is said to be slowing down in Lake Mead recently, due in part to the fact that Lake Powell upstream is short-stopping some of it.

The sediment that free-flowing rivers carry, normally erodes the river channel and increases its capabilities for carrying flood waters. Dams hold the sediment back, it builds up, and the process is reversed.

As explained by geographer H. F. Garner in *Scientific American* in an article "Rivers In the Making," the sedimentation of rivers is a problem with which engineers have never successfully coped. There is no known way to flush accumulations of sediment through dams and out of reservoirs. As the reservoirs fill up, their value for flood control diminishes and the danger of floods increases.

One of the most searching studies of benefit-cost calculations came to the attention of the Congressional

Subcommittee on Irrigation and Reclamation of the House Committee on Interior and Insular Affairs, during the celebrated debates on whether or not to dam the Grand Canyon. The Bureau of Reclamation's calculations were reviewed by economists Dr. Alan P. Carlin and Dr. William E. Hoehn of Santa Monica, California. As an aid to the Sierra Club efforts to block this giant construction project, and as a public service, these skilled professionals donated their own time to the study. The results were not comforting to the Bureau of Reclamation. It became relatively clear that the benefit-cost ratio for the Grand Canyon dams was actually less than one-to-one.

For the benefit of the committee members, some of whom were hostile to any opposition to the Bureau's plan, the two economists proceeded to analyze the Bureau points, one at a time. They explained that the reason for the differences between their calculations and those of the Bureau was that the government planners had relied on, ". . . a number of economically questionable procedures. . . ." One of these, the California economists explained, was an interest rate too low to be realistic. The Bureau interest rate was based on a paper known as Senate Document 97, the existence of which proves that Congress has not been above creating economic crutches on which its builders and diggers can lean. Senate Document 97, created in 1962, has since been attacked by numerous professional economists. You find the proper interest rate on a proposed water project, says Document 97, by looking at the rates paid by the government on outstanding interest-bearing marketable securities with maturity of fifteen years or more. Instead of taking into account either current interest rates, or the trend as it would appear to predict future interest rates, this procedure allows government workers to utilize interest rates that are largely matters of history.

As a professor of economics, Dr. William J. Baumol of Princeton University, told a 1967 Subcommittee on Economy in Government, "When I first came across this, several months ago, I mentioned it without comment to several economists to get their reaction. They were completely incredulous. They just could not believe that such a procedure was employed anywhere." Of the three eminent economists testifying before the subcommittee, Representative William S. Moorhead of Pennsylvania asked, "Am I correct in assuming that all three of you agree that the procedure as described in this Document 97 is wrong?"

To this Professor Baumol answered, "Certainly."

"Yes," said Dr. Jacob A. Stockfisch of the Institute of Defense Analysis.

"Yes," replied Morton Kamien, associate professor of economics, Carnegie-Mellon University.

Senate Document 97 permits the builders and diggers the luxury of a ridiculously low rate of interest compared with rates cautious private investors would use.

At the time the interest rate commonly used on reclamation projects was 3⅛ per cent. Dr. Stockfisch, as well as other economists, claimed a more realistic figure would be 10 per cent (before taxes). "Does it shake you at all," asked Senator William Proxmire, long-time foe of government waste in water projects, "that this would probably terminate the government investment in Reclamation projects?"

"Not one bit," Dr. Stockfisch replied. "I think we probably are investing relatively too much in water."

"After all that has been written about the evaluation of water projects," testified Dr. Hoehn and Dr. Carlin, before a congressional committee, "it would be naïve to assume that the thinking represented by Senate Document 97 and its application to the Grand Canyon controversy results entirely from ignorance of economic principles; much more can be explained by the political realities of the situation. The most important of these realities is the mutuality of interest between members of Congress anxious to obtain projects beneficial to their constituents and federal water agencies looking for more business. Loose evaluation criteria serve the ends of both, as does the practice of having the agencies themselves apply these criteria to individual projects."

At a more realistic interest rate of 5 per cent, the benefit-cost ratios nose-dived to 0.52 for the Hualapai Dam and 0.61 for the Marble Canyon structure.

Both the Corps of Engineers and the Bureau of Reclamation are famous for shaving cost figures. One day in 1962, when Congress was deliberating the wisdom of going ahead with a Kansas irrigation system known as the Glen Elder Project, Senator William Proxmire rose to add to the record some startling conclusions.

Glen Elder dated back to 1944. With the country in the greatest war in its history, and the need for increased production, including agricultural production, evident, the Glen Elder Dam promised irrigation water to increase the country's stores of grain. The legislation authorizing the project was the Pick-Sloane Act which lumped Glen Elder in with a long list of other projects. It was but one part of a gigantic plan for developing the Missouri Valley.

Once authorized, such a project may be held in abeyance until the responsible agency needs work, or some member of Congress urges its completion. Eighteen years passed. Glen Elder was up now, in 1962, for consideration as one of the projects to be granted funds for construction. But the picture of need had changed drastically. The war was over, and instead of food shortages, the country was struggling with a gigantic grain surplus. The demand and supply picture in itself can change and the current surpluses should not, of themselves, rule out the advisability of the Glen Elder Project.

Senator Proxmire, however, was especially concerned about the rising cost of the project. Originally, promised at $17 million, the cost had risen to $76 million, and in later years it continued spiraling. Meanwhile, the number of acres it was designed to irrigate was lowered from 26,000 to 21,000, which increased still more the cost of each acre reclaimed. As the Senator from Wisconsin explained to his fellow legislators, the per acre cost of irrigation of this land had eventually risen to $1729 which was more than the irrigated land was worth.

What of the old Reclamation promise that the water users would repay the project costs? Senator Proxmire explained that, over a fifty-year period, they would pay back only $191 per acre. But Congress approved the appropriation, and Glen Elder Dam was underway.

For more examples of underestimated costs, the building agencies have only to look into their own files. The Sacramento River canal was originally estimated, when authorized in 1946, to be available for $10,742,000. At that price the potential dollar return was said to be about equal to the cost. By 1966, according to the Corps of Engineers' Annual Report, the price tag including maintenance was adjusted to $52,634,122—five times the original estimate.

When its congressional advocates were staging their hard sell, the infamous Arkansas River navigation project was said to be available at a mere $435 million. That was also 1946. By 1967, with the project only partly completed, the estimated price had climbed to $1.2 *billion*.

Meanwhile federal dollars continued to fall like autumn leaves on the surface of the "Beautiful Ohio."

This major inland stream was blessed in 1910 by a congressional authorization for $73 million worth of improvements. The figure was supposed to build the navigation structures needed on the river from Cairo to Pittsburgh, a distance of 981 miles. When President Hoover journeyed to Cincinnati to dedicate the completed system in 1929, the cost had climbed to $100 million. But the new dams so increased the suitability of the river for the subsidized barge traffic that they were soon overtaxed. Barges grew bigger. Instead of 600-foot locks, there was need for locks 1200 feet long. The Corps of Engineers then worked out plans for a brand-new system of nineteen high-lift dams and locks to replace the former forty-six dams. It is to be completed around 1980. By 1966 the Ohio River navigation works had cost $788 million, all based on the original project.

It is frequent practice for the Bureau of Reclamation and the Army Corps of Engineers, when figuring the value of a proposed project, to ignore any losses that might result. Some of the losses are incalculable because they destroy such natural wonders as wilderness areas or river valleys. Losses that could be more easily computed may also be ignored. There is a glaring example in the celebrated case of the dams which the Bureau of Reclamation proposed for the Grand Canyon. Economists noted that the Bureau chose to ignore the evaporation losses of 100,000 acre-feet of water annually from the proposed reservoirs. The benefit-cost figures allowed this water a value of zero, but in the thirsty West no such quantity of impounded water has a true value of zero. To replace this water, as they planned to do eventually with water brought in from the Columbia River, would cost a minimum of $70 per acre-foot. As the Sierra Club noted, ". . . this subsidy amounts to an additional $7 million per year."

The Bureau of Reclamation had chosen to overlook this loss.

Economist Dr. Robert H. Haveman published, in 1965, his scholarly analysis of federal water projects in ten southern states following World War II. His conclusions should be carefully reviewed by anyone in a position to allocate public funds. Of the 147 projects for which he could obtain benefit-cost figures, 63 proved, when tested against sophisticated economic techniques, to be such poor investments that they should not have been undertaken in the first place. These wasteful projects were to cost $1,169,000,000, which was fully 44 per cent of the funds allocated to the 147 projects. This, as Dr. Haveman pointed out, constitutes a misallocation of national resources, and economic waste.

Economically, the water management projects constructed by the Corps and the Bureau of Reclamation are so riddled with obvious waste that economy-minded taxpayers should long since have cut these programs back to sound and justifiable levels. As the programs have grown of their own momentum and without any nationwide planning, they have consumed billions of the national treasury and destroyed increasingly valuable natural areas for all time.

In 1964 Senator Proxmire made a study of 380 water resources projects. "These projects," he wrote, "involve total costs of over $16 billion. Yet 220 of these projects costing $7.5 billion could not be justified by normal business standards. The 220 projects have been selected because the estimated benefits, according to the Corps and Bureau, are less than double the anticipated costs. I have consistently found," the Senator added, "that projects with an alleged benefit-cost ratio of less than two to one provide returns less than their cost. Costs of public works are invariably much greater than originally estimated because of poor estimates and inflationary pressures. On the other hand, true benefits to the nation typically run way below agency estimates. Opposition to this pure blubber in the pork barrel is increasing in the Congress and the nation."

ONE FOR THE ROAD

Like their brethren who specialize in dams, canals, and drainage ditches, highway engineers have also learned that by careful grooming they can give a benefit-cost ratio a magic touch. Such calculations may appear sound until they fall under the critical and experienced examining eyes of a professional civil engineer. This is what happened when the Colorado Department of Highways planned to run Interstate 70 along the Gore Range-Eagle Nest primitive area. The alternative to this 16.5-mile route that would mar a wild and beautiful mountain scene, was a 27.3-mile route largely along the existing Vail Pass Route. When conservationists arose to object to violation of the wilderness, the highway engineers pointed to their benefit-cost calculations to prove the economy of their choice.

DESIGN AND COST CHARACTERISTICS OF ALTERNATE FREEWAY ROUTES*

	Vail Pass Route	Red Buffalo Route
Route Length	27.3 miles	16.5 miles
Average Grade	3.1%	5.1%
Design Speed	50 mph	50 mph
Initial Cost Roadway	$17,514,000	$19,079,000

*Source: Colorado Department of Highways, Interstate Highway Location Study, Dillon to Dowd, Colorado, May, 1964 revised April, 1966.

Pavement	2,650,000	1,652,000
Twin tunnel	—	41,211,000
Right-of-way	2,639,000	1,153,000
Total	$22,803,000	$63,095,000
Initial Cost Converted to Annual Basis, C	$ 1,112,000	$ 2,708,000
Annual Maintenance Cost, M	$ 102,000	$ 200,000
Total Annual Highway Cost, C+M	$ 1,214,000	$ 2,908,000
Annual Road User Cost	$11,750,000	$ 8,457,000

At this stage Dr. Dennis R. Neuzil, former instructor in civil engineering at the University of Colorado, member of the American Society of Civil Engineers and the Institute of Traffic Engineers, and an Assistant Professor of Civil Engineering at the University of Delaware, began looking more critically at the highway planners' logic. As for cost, the highway planners are concerned only with the actual price of building and the cost of maintaining the road. Intangible losses or benefits are usually ignored.

But as Dr. Neuzil wrote in the Sierra Club Bulletin, the route the engineers proposed for the I-70 project to follow, although shorter, would cost in the end almost three times as much as the Vail Pass route. The wilderness route included a $41-million tunnel. The higher cost, the engineers claimed, was justified because the savings of the shorter route would return the investment. Dr. Neuzil pointed out two weaknesses in their figures.

First there was the old interest rate loophole. The 3.5 interest rate assigned the Colorado project helped account for its healthy-looking 1.94 to 1 benefit-cost ratio. Such an interest rate was, however, unrealistic in this day and age. Where highway funds are obtained from the highway user, his investment in highways should be comparable to earnings he might expect from the same money privately invested. The interest rate the motorist pays to finance his car, Dr. Neuzil suggested, might be a good *minimum* rate of return to expect from highway investments, and 6 to 8 per cent would come far closer to such a figure than the Highway Department's 3.5 per cent. "The validity of a benefit-cost ratio," he explained, "may be called into question whenever an interest rate of less than 6 per cent was used."

He found too that the Highway Department had assigned the Red Buffalo route a life expectancy of between forty and sixty years, longer than economists can justify. "The highway engineer who assumes that current technology will serve acceptably forty to sixty years from now is simply naïve," said Dr. Neuzil. Traffic forecasts cannot be considered reliable for more than twenty years ahead.

In addition, he noted that the department had failed to take into account the greater cost of operating truck traffic on the proposed Red Buffalo route as compared with the Vail Pass route, in spite of the fact that the Red Buffalo route is much steeper. Although steepness of grade may not be a major factor in the cost of car operation, it quickly becomes a factor of increasing cost for the big highway transport companies. Figuring the potential savings for the shorter route through the wilderness Dr. Neuzil concluded that truckers would save $40,000. The Highway Department, using its own methods, had claimed a saving of $660,000.

The significance of such variations comes into sharp focus when they are totaled. Using the properly adjusted truck savings figures, a realistic 6 per cent interest rate and even a thirty-year life expectancy, the benefit-cost ratio comes out not the 1.94 to 1 claimed by the Highway Department, but 0.90 to 1. Consequently, the Red Buffalo route appears uneconomical even without attempting to figure in the damage it would inflict on the wilderness region through which it would pass. Because there is no formula for assigning a dollar value to scenery, the building agencies blithely give it a value of zero. Obviously, however, scenery has a real value to the travel industry and to people.

Meanwhile, the more readily measurable economic losses to the nation are staggering. We pour great sums of the national treasury into projects that hold no genuine legitimate promise of paying off. This takes funds from worthy projects and puts the builders and diggers into the position of depressing our long-range national growth.

PART III

"Each generation has only a temporary rendezvous with the land."

Stewart L. Udall

10. The Earth Eaters

For three miles our car labored over a dirt road newly cut around the steep slopes. Once a huge truck labored around the bend toward us and inched down the mountainside carrying twenty tons of coal. We waited at one side to let it pass. The driver did not wave or smile. This was not a public road and he probably felt that we had no legal right on the mountain. But I wanted to see the active mining operation then gnawing away at the mountaintop hidden from the sight of the world below.

A mile farther, we rounded a point and saw the story written in yellow scars on the mountainsides. The top of a mountain should, one feels, be an inspiring peak with great sweeping views and invigorating air. But this was the inside of hell. Benches of yellow earth followed the contours. Miles of these continuous yellow cuts stretched away and out of sight around the mountains. Artificial cliffs of crumbling rock had replaced the ancient hardwood forests. Great piles of debris had been pushed over the edge of the cuts to slide and crash down on the slopes below.

My companion was a mountain man. This was his country. Friends of his drove some of the coal trucks. But like many another mountain man, he did not like what he had brought me to see that morning. Next we came upon a scene where three men stood around a bulldozer on the bench below. One of the men hailed us and began climbing the rubble-strewn bank. The cameras hanging from my neck felt heavy, and very conspicuous. It was obvious to this man that we had not climbed the mountain to organize any "friends of the strip miner" group.

"Where you fellows going?"

"Just thought we might walk out here and make some pictures."

"I just think you better not. We're blastin' out there and you might get covered up." He did not smile. "You just better go on back outa here. You haven't any right to be up here making pictures. We don't need you up here."

In those mountains, men have traditionally come and gone as they pleased. Mountain men don't take lightly to being "ordered off" by other men. We went back down the mountain, but my companion, who had known the miner all his life, was quiet and withdrawn. In these hills, feuds have started with less provocation.

But we had seen what we came to see. We had seen one more of the places where the strip miners are, at this moment, tearing away the mountains, in perhaps the most shameful case of permanent land abuse on the North American continent. It is in the nation's coal fields, where the black mineral is taken by stripping, that man has proved that his technological ability can develop faster than his sense of social or ecological responsibility.

Depending on the steepness of the mined land, a stripping operation may be classified as either area strip mining or contour strip mining. On the mountainous lands the coal-stripping machines start at an outcropping and work around the slopes in ribbonlike contour operations, digging back into the hills as far as they can, until the overburden becomes too thick to move profitably. On the more level or gentle rolling lands the mining machines frequently begin with a box or trench cut to the coal below, then they uncover the entire area economically and efficiently. In either type of strip mining there can be serious reclamation problems, and usually are. In addition to area and contour strip mining, engineers in recent times have developed a third method of reaching coal formerly out of reach beneath the mountains of Appalachia; they drill it out with gigantic augers that riddle the hillsides with rows of holes.

In the same family of destructive industrial processes are the open-pit mines where workmen quarry such minerals as limestone, sandstone, marble, sand, and gravel. Such mining operations seldom arouse the opposition the coal strip miners face because they disturb relatively smaller areas and provide work longer. They may last half a century or more which is in sharp contrast to what happens in the coal fields. Coal seams are seldom more than a few feet thick. Seams of bituminous coal mined in one recent year averaged 5.1 feet thick. Consequently, the stripping machines can move rapidly over large areas.

Surface mining also includes the processes of dredging and hydraulic mining for gold, sand, and gravel. These operations frequently leave spoil banks and feed polluting sediment into public waters. In all of these processes men have been too little concerned with the condition of the land they leave behind. "It was and still is," Secretary of the Interior Stewart L. Udall, has said, "accepted practice to mine as cheaply as possible the deposits that are most accessible and provide the greatest profit to the producer. This preoccupation with short-term gain too frequently has ignored the long-term social costs involved—the silted streams, the acid-laden waters, and the wasteland left by surface mining."

The Appalachian Regional Development Act enacted by Congress in 1965 handed to Secretary of the Interior Stewart L. Udall, the task of studying the scourge of surface mining across Appalachia and then delivering to President Johnson a program to reclaim those vast acreages left barren behind the diggers. Secretary Udall brought to the task the combined talents of specialists from many bureaus within his department. Into the mine fields across the country went geologists, biologists, soils experts, mining authorities, water pollution specialists, and others who could help appraise the problem. It was the first national effort to see where the country stands in terms of land use by surface miners. Questionnaires went out to all states. Governors were asked to help obtain the completed forms from thousands of mine operators. The Secretary's committee consulted with state officials, mine-industry representatives, and conservation organizations. By random sampling, the committee selected 693 surface mining sites which they then visited for further detailed study.

When brought together, the resulting report held up to a rich and productive land a picture of ugliness. "Surface mining," said the report, "frequently shocks the sensibilities, not so much by what is done as by the sheer magnitude of man's accomplishments. He literally has moved mountains, and some of his surface excavations are so vast as to resemble craters on the moon. Surface mining destroys the protective vegetative cover, and the soil and rock overlying the mineral deposit is frequently left in massive piles cast onto adjoining land. The result is a drastic reshaping of the surface, an alteration of normal surface and subsurface drainage patterns. Square miles of land may be turned over to depths of 100 feet or more and valleys rimmed by mile after mile of contour benches. Massive landslides have blocked streams and highways, waters have been polluted by acid and sediment, land areas isolated, and economic and esthetic values seriously impaired."

Such devastated areas command little respect from anyone. Secretary Udall's report revealed that, "Although mine operators had generally removed all their buildings and equipment from abandoned strip mine sites, a third of the visited areas were being used illegally . . . by the public to discard garbage, rubble, junked vehicles, and construction materials. Such misuse endangers public health and safety . . . In addition mine fires, which cost the nation millions of dollars annually, are often started by burning trash and other materials in abandoned coal-strip pits."

The report further pointed out the effect of strip mining on surrounding lands, and said the entire landscape is disfigured where one acre in ten is laid waste. In front of the machines rises the high wall, the artificial cliff the machines create. The earth is shoved to the mountainside and pushed over the edge, and where it goes from there, whether into forests, highways, streams or yards, is more often than not in the hands of God and gravity. Wet weather and frost frequently loosens the waste material and sends it down in the mud slides of which mountain people in Appalachia live in constant dread.

In June, 1966, Secretary Udall told the nation, "The problems related to strip and surface mining have grown, and if left unchecked, will continue to expand with our increasing population and higher standard of living."

There are, the government investigators learned, 25 000 miles of such strip mine cuts along the mountain contours. Piled along the lip of the contour benches are 18,000 miles of spoil banks. The remaining 7000 miles of cuts have had the earth pushed off the bench onto the steep slopes below. Where the earth is heaped along the outer edges of the cuts, it often traps water in pockets between the spoil and the high wall, then seepage from the exposed coal seams pollutes it with acids, to form reservoirs of death-dealing chemicals. These are periodically flushed down the mountain and into the streams below by the heavy rains. Massive slides have already been visited upon 1700 miles of these steep slopes, including some that were considered "reclaimed."

How fast is surface mining adding to the present acreage of disturbed land? At the time of the government study the figure was in excess of 150,000 acres annually. Of this, less than one-third was being reclaimed. Surface mining activities, meanwhile, were expanding rapidly. By 1980 more than five million acres of America will have been damaged by surface mining.

Although strip mining may be at its most destructive and dramatic in Appalachia, it is by no means limited to those grand old mountains which the early settlers found rich in game and timber and solitude. There has been strip or open-pit mining to some extent in practically every state. According to Secretary Udall's well-documented report, "About 15,000 active surface mines, producing some 50 mineral commodities, account for approximately 83 per cent of the total coal and crude-ore tonnage mined in the United States, including . . . one-third of the coal." In one phosphate mining operation in southern Idaho, the high walls cut across the migration routes of elk and mule deer and brought concentrations of hunters to those points where the animals moving down to their historic wintering grounds were forced to cross the open mining areas.

By 1965 our strip mining operations had disturbed—which is a gentle word the mining interests frequently substitute for "destroyed"—3.2 million acres of the American landscape. And 66 per cent of these mined lands lay barren and unreclaimed. Of the 34 per cent "reclaimed" almost half had been treated, not by man who destroyed it, but by the forces of nature. Of all the lands so far stripped, industry had made reclamation efforts on slightly more than 16 per cent. The remainder was abandoned and left for the rest of us to treat and patch and repair if we can.

And the coal-stripping industry is in its youth. Vast stores of coal remain, to promise lasting wealth to the coal merchants, and continued devastation to the land around us. In the Kentucky mountains alone, where 119,000 acres have been "disturbed," Edward T. Breathitt, strip mine opponent and ex-governor, has said that scarcely one per cent of the coal has so far been removed. There are, he told some of the mountain people at one meeting, about 10 million acres yet to be mined out.

Strip mining is so descriptively named that the coal operators prefer to call it "open-pit" mining. But, in fact, the earth is stripped to uncover the coal, which is then loosened with explosives and scooped up to be hauled away. In the mountainous regions, it is where these beds of coal come close to the surface that machinery can reach it for open-pit mining. The coal buried deepest in the heart of the mountains can only be reached by deep shaft mines.

Commercial strip mining was born a century or more ago. Like many another infant, this new mining method carried little resemblance to the giant it would become. Near Pittsburg, Kansas, J. N. Hodges and A. J. Armil made history, of sorts, in 1877, when they replaced their mule-drawn scrapers with a chugging steam shovel, the first power-driven shovel ever used in a strip mining operation. Here was a marvel of the decade. Belching black coal smoke and shuddering on its foundation, the laboring power-driven bucket pawed at the earth in its clumsy efforts to clear off the ten-foot overburden, and expose the three-foot seam of coal. But the earth so resisted the futile efforts of the pioneering little shovel that the operation failed, and the strip miners gave up their dream.

Until 1911 the early coal-stripping efforts had all employed machines intended for other purposes. That year a manufacturer of shovels put to work in Illinois, near Danville, the first modern power shovel made especially for coal stripping. The dipper riding at the end of its 65-foot boom would lift three and a half yards of earth at a time, and the manufacturer proudly announced that this was the "largest coal-stripping shovel in the world." The clue to the future of the stripping industry was bigness.

The railroad tracks on which early shovels moved were taken away as the new models stood on their own crawler-type tracks. Bucket sizes grew until by the early 1940s they could lift thirty-five yards of earth in a single bite. The machines became taller and their booms longer, making it feasible to move earth farther and take away increasingly heavy layers of overburden. But these giants of their day were erector-set toys compared to some of the machines about to be turned loose in the coal fields.

Near Cadiz, Ohio, in the hill country where strip mining had already scarred the slopes for several decades, there went to work, in 1956, the first of a genre known among proud machinery makers as "the super shovels." This steel beast was called the "Mountaineer." But instead of climbing mountains, its specialty was eating them, with a spoon capable of lifting sixty yards at a bite. Other and bigger shovels were soon to follow. The coal operators seeking to meet the competition for low-production costs and towering profits were investing millions of dollars in these coal machines. And with each step up in size of shovels, the operators were capable of digging into a coal seam where the depth of overburden had made earlier stripping operations economically impractical.

In the rolling land of Coshocton County, Ohio, the Columbus and Southern Ohio Electric Company installed, at a cost of $2.7 million its "Coal Chief," a power shovel capable of biting off 105 tons of earth at once. The boom and dipper handle enabled the operator to pick up the earth and drop it again as far as the length of a football field away.

Constructing the Coal Chief was much like building a huge mobile factory. Its parts arrived in a string of sixty-five railroad cars, and workmen labored for half a year to assemble the shovel. Said the new owner, "The side of a hill in the coal field was cut down to provide space for assembling this giant shovel."

Records for bigness of man-made machines fall fast, and soon other shovels would topple the Coal Chief from its promontory. One was installed by Peabody Coal Company in its sprawling strip mine holdings near Paradise, Kentucky. This giant among giants rises as high as a twenty-story skyscraper. It arrived in three hundred railroad cars and, when assembled, equaled the weight of six thousand automobiles. One man handles this monster with fewer controls than needed to drive an automobile. Six stories above ground he sits in a soft chair in his glass enclosed, air-conditioned cab, which he reaches by riding an elevator to work.

Behind this monstrous creation lies the desolate, unsightly landscape that has become typical of the strip mine lands in the relatively level coal fields. Here strip mining enabled local people to brag that Muehlenberg County is the largest single coal-producing county in the United States. The coal goes to feed a giant new TVA power plant whose towering smokestacks are landmarks for miles around.

Sometimes the proud and publicity conscious strip mine owners boast of their giant earth-eating devices as major regional tourist attractions. There can be no question that the big shovels are impressive engineering and mechanical accomplishments. Wide-eyed visitors, secure in the comfort of their automobiles, wend their way through the man-fashioned badlands to stop eventually in the shadow of the towering steel giant. Awestruck, and with the first "gee whiz" frozen on their lips, fascinated sightseers marvel anew at the skills of the species to which they belong. "In the course of a year's digging on the Panama Canal," they are told, "all of the seventy-seven shovels employed to scoop out the Big Ditch could move only half as much earth as this single strip mining machine."

Coal stripping was well underway here some years ago, and broad fields lay yellow and eroding beneath the Kentucky sun when the highway engineers announced their chosen route of the Kentucky Turnpike. The big dual-lane highway with its wide median strip was to stretch for miles through the heart of these strip mine leavings. The company made such efforts at reclamation as the Kentucky strip mine laws necessitated, but it could not hide the scars. Between the spindly pine seedlings run myriads of gullies of infinite designs and depths. I have heard state reclamation workers, as well as coal company people, point to these pitiful pine plantings flanking the Kentucky Turnpike as evidence of good reclamation.

Strip mining in flat or rolling areas is highly efficient. The machines uncover the flat coal seam a band at a time, until they have removed all of the coal up to their property line. In such lands the thickness of the overburden is likely to be fairly uniform, and all of it shallow enough to fall victim to the earth-moving equipment.

In the sharply rising slopes of the Appalachians, however, the story may be entirely different. The flat seam of coal often crops out of the mountainside or comes quite close to the surface in a black band that lies like the icing between two layers of cake. The layer of earth over it however, rises to a peak or ridge. The coal miner may get only a single ribbonlike cut around the contour of the mountain. Standing straight behind this cut is the yellow crumbling high wall, sometimes nearly a hundred feet high. The operator has reached the limits of his machinery, and has removed from the mountain only a fraction of the richness that lies there.

A West Virginia operator, some years ago, obtained a huge diamond-headed steel auger, sixteen inches in diameter. He attached it to the drilling machine he used for boring holes for blasting, set the machine in motion, and watched the auger begin drilling straight back into the black face of the exposed coal seam. The auger bored into the seam of coal, breaking the mineral free and drawing it back out of the hole. This pioneering idea soon spread to other mines. Machine companies began working on bigger and better coal augers. The strip miner had now added to his arsenal a new means of violating the mountains. Now giant augers drilling their rows of holes around the mountains bring out more than ten million tons of coal a year in a method that can be fantastically profitable.

Coal augers range in size from sixteen inches to seven feet in diameter. Some are capable of boring out as much as 25½ tons of coal per minute and dropping it onto conveyor belts on either side of the machine to speed the transporting of the coal from the holes. Some machines drive two, three, or more augers into the hill at once in varying combinations of size to match the thickness of the coal seam.

Close behind the stripping shovels, the augers move onto the bench to take up their positions, before weathering and age have weakened and pitted the high wall. The augers can be driven as far as two hundred and twenty feet straight back into the coal seam. Then they attack the seam from the opposite side gradually removing more and more of the mountain's foundation. So economically efficient is augering, however, that abandoned strip mines are sometimes reopened years later to the big drills. In places where coal might not have been economically mined previously, improved marketing and machinery may bring the miners back in some future year. Scarcely a mountain is ever safe if coal lies anywhere beneath it.

Augers also permit miners to open up seams on slopes previously not mined by stripping. In such virgin mine fields, augers may leave as much as 80 per cent of the coal. Frequently, however, they have so abused the mountain that deep shaft mines will be impossible there by any methods now known since the augers have chewed through the areas that would be needed for mine supports. Air entering the seam through the auger holes causes decay and weakens the coal. Weight from above helps to crush the weakened structure, and the remaining wealth of coal is effectively sealed in its tomb, perhaps forever, beyond the reach of shaft operations that might otherwise have recovered it when economics demanded. The augers in these cases become tools for scalping off the easy profits without concern for wasted resources or future needs.

Along with more efficient mining equipment come new ways to transport coal to the power plants. Self-powered trains of large capacity will haul 35,000 tons instead of 7000 to 8000 tons. They can be locked in position, turned over and emptied without uncoupling. Coal also travels by water on big river barges, and it can be powdered, mixed with water, and pumped through pipelines. In other cases, power generators can be installed near the mines and the "coal" shipped as kilowatts. Meanwhile, highly efficient power plant furnaces have been invented, capable of burning crushed coal that does not even require cleaning, thus further increasing the market for low-quality coal.

In due time level lands stripped and then returned to their former contours may return to crop or timber production. But it is another, and sadder, story in the mountains. Often I think of that desolate mountain we climbed in eastern Kentucky. There was no beauty, only ruin. Even as they speak of reclaiming these homemade badlands, men know that the devastation inflicted upon the Appalachians is too great to repair. No man can put the mountain back.

11. The Strip Mine March

On a pleasant morning in early summer I sat in the back row of the chambers of the Kentucky Court of Appeals, which is the state's supreme court. The richly paneled walls of the luxurious room seemed a long way removed from the devastated landscape which was the subject of litigation that morning.

Directly in front of me sat Helen and LeRoy Morgan and a neighbor who had come to Frankfort with them from the mountain coal fields where they live. The Martin's ten-acre property on Lotts Creek was the subject under discussion. The entire coal industry was interested in seeing the court find in favor of the companies that were inching toward Morgan's property in that steep valley. Meanwhile, those citizens who had struggled so long against the strip miners in Kentucky were well aware that this could be a key case in finally breaking the death grip of the predatory industry on the rest of eastern Kentucky. It was no ordinary case.

Attorney for the Martins was the tall and eloquent Harry M. Caudill, the Kentuckian the strip miners hated most. His compelling book, *Night Comes to the Cumberlands*, had stated the case against the Kentucky coal industry and political system so well that he could never be forgiven.

The subject before the black-robed court on this occasion was a strange archaic legal document known as the "broad form deed." Throughout the Appalachians, this broad form deed became the instrument that would enable coal companies to wreck farms, homes, and villages without worrying about paying for damages. It said, in effect, that the owner was selling for all time, the minerals beneath his land. Furthermore, the holder of the mineral rights could legally advance on the property at any future time to take the minerals. He could utilize the standing timber for his mine props. He was not to be held liable for polluting streams, destroying buildings, roads, or farm fields.

Many a pioneering family in the Appalachians was so taken in by the smooth-talking agents who visited them seeking mineral rights in the late 1800s and early 1900s, that they signed over their mineral rights for twenty-five cents to fifty cents an acre. Often the deeds were signed with an "X," beside which was noted "His mark." The deed forms were even printed by the companies seeking the coal-mining rights. Although property owners signing the deed might not receive a copy, copies were registered in the court houses of eastern Kentucky. There they can be found today, binding the unfortunate signers and their descendants to the letter of the agreement which is, in effect, a guillotine hanging over entire valleys.

Under the broad form deed those who come to extract the coal can cross the line fence legally. They are allowed to mine the coal by any method they choose. Time after time farm families who have spent decades taking a meager harvest from the forest-rimmed hollows, have watched the advancing bulldozers tearing at the hillsides where they have raised their families. The courts and the broad form deed have rendered them impotent.

Behind their machines the coal miners have left great masses of sterile yellow earth. During the wet seasons the barren soil banks absorb massive weights of water. The softening mud begins to move down the mountain. It flows over homes, highways, cemeteries, gardens, and cornfields. And the coal companies causing the ruin have been held free of damages because they did not inflict the damage "maliciously."

The broad form deed was not peculiar to Kentucky. This scourge was visited on the hills of West Virginia, Pennsylvania, Tennessee, and other Appalachian states as well. But in every state except Kentucky, the courts have long since ruled that this legal instrument should no longer leave the owner of mineral rights free of damages to the owner of the surface. At the time these deeds were drawn up, the only method used to extract coal from the hills commercially was the shaft mine. Men went into the bowels of the earth through handmade tunnels, blasting, picking, and shoveling coal while leaving most of the surface untouched, to go on growing timber and wildlife as it had since the beginning of time. Strip mining had not yet been conceived. The first mineral purchasers, when they bought the rights to the riches beneath those Kentucky hills, obviously did not foresee the day when the entire tops and sides of the hills would be removed to expose coal to daylight. To be sure, the purchasers of mineral rights had fully intended to gather great wealth to themselves through their broad form deeds, but their intent had been to take the valuable coal by deep shaft mining, because in those times this was the only way known to get it out of the earth. On the logic of this argument, one state after the other across Appalachia ruled that the holder of mineral rights did not also hold the right to destroy the surface along with its trees, grass, water, and wildlife. Kentucky was an exception because of the simple political fact that in the eastern Kentucky coal fields, the coal mine owners also owned the courthouse. The little man could not fight "the company." Included among those who usually answered first to the companies were the high sheriff and his kinfolk, the county commissioners, judges, and even the jailer. The sheriff's deputies were sometimes on coal company payrolls, and the companies would hire extra deputies if there should be a threat of union organizers coming into the hills.

This was the age of company towns. Miners, forced to rent from their employers and make their purchases, often at exorbitant prices, at the company-owned stores, were held in perpetual bondage, unless their health failed, in which case they were usually evicted. Although the company towns began to disappear and mine owners assumed more enlightened attitudes, remnants of the power structure persist today in the strip mine fields. It is seen in consistent court rulings favoring the companies and the holders of broad form deeds, and in the freedom with which overloaded coal trucks are permitted to speed around the roads of Appalachia.

Occasionally, the Kentucky Bureau of Roads will move into an eastern Kentucky coal county with a set of portable scales. They know in advance that every coal truck on the roads, except the empty ones, will be overloaded. But suddenly coal trucks no longer come down the road. Being equipped with two-way radio the truck drivers have alerted each other before the scales are well in place. For a couple of days the idle patrolman sits beside his unused scales while truckers blithely detour around the scene until the operation is called off. Or, if the truckers should be caught by surprise, the local court, more often than not, quickly dismisses the cases. One court once dismissed 121 such cases in a single day. The judge's reasoning was that "These men have to make a living."

This seasoned attitude which places the power organization above the rights and welfare of the people, or the preservation of the landscape, reaches to the legislative halls in the state capitol in Frankfort.

In recent years the Kentucky legislature has attracted an increasingly higher caliber of representative, but the age of the pay-off is far from dead. "With $10,000," one Kentucky lawmaker said, "You could get the Kentucky legislature to repeal the Ten Commandments." In spite of the gradually changing attitude, the broad form deed hangs on in Kentucky's hills.

Perhaps the best that Harry Caudill and the commonwealth attorney, Dave Schneider, could expect for their clients, the Martins, was a ruling forcing strip miners to pay damages to surface owners.

The Martins must have heard all the coal company arguments a dozen times before, but they still could not quite believe what the court was being told. "The land in most cases where it is strip mined," one of the attorneys intoned, "is vastly improved." Mrs. Martin shook her head in disbelief. "They should come out and see how it's vastly improved," she said.

"And they oughta tell the truth once," her neighbor added.

A few hundred yards up the hollow from the Martin home, the county road was, at the moment, covered with an earthslide from a strip mine. The only way the school bus could reach homes beyond the slide was by a forty-mile detour. Up and down the hollow, the coal strippers had laid the mountains open as if the earth were undergoing some massive post-mortem.

By this time the Martins were controversial figures in their own right. LeRoy Martin, a tall, slender mountaineer with a burr haircut and loosely fitting suit, had long been a schoolteacher in Cordova High School. In addition, he drove a passenger vehicle bringing some of his high school students down out of the steepest trunk roads to the main highways every day. But in their spare time the Martins had organized their mountain neighbors into the Appalachian Association to Save the Land and People, a group that became a burr beneath the strip miner's saddle. Here was no outside agitator arguing for the rights of the mountain people. The people themselves were finding spokesmen, who could not be bought out.

"All we want to do," Mrs. Martin said, "is save our homes." They feel that, in the mountains, coal miners should go back to the shaft mining method and that the strip mining that destroys the hills, and the broad form deed permitting it, have no place in their modern world.

Some weeks after their court appearance in Frankfort, the Kentucky Court of Appeals upheld the mine operators. They were free to go on taking coal under the broad form mineral-rights deeds without paying any compensation for damages to those who own the surface. One saddened eastern Kentucky farmer said it gave the operators a license to drive bulldozers through living rooms.

What most Americans do not realize is the extent to which each of us pays taxes for the mineral industries. As if it were not enough to see the land desecrated, we permit this industry the sweeping advantages of little-known federal laws which actually excuse strip miners and mineral deed owners from paying taxes on large portions of their income.

The coal industry is permitted a depletion allowance of 10 per cent. This federal law permits a coal mine owner to keep 10 per cent of his net, tax free, or not more than 50 per cent of his gross. Similar laws benefit the extractors of numerous minerals ranging from oil to asbestos. On oil the depletion allowance is an unbelievable and unjustifiable 27½ per cent. According to the study of a Joint Committee Report on the Federal Revenue System, this enables a person investing in an extractive industry to recover tax free, ". . . virtually the full amount of his investment in a mineral

property often in the year the outlays are made . . ."
After that he can go ahead and continue to claim
percentage-depletion allowances which ". . . bear no
relationship to the amount of his investment. Accord-
ingly, the law may permit tax-free recovery of his
capital costs several times over."

There is on record, as the Secretary of the Treasury
pointed out some years ago before the House Ways
and Means Committee, one case of a taxpayer with a
five-year earning of $14.3 million, on which only
$80,000 was paid in federal income tax. Entirely legal,
this minuscule payment amounted to a rate of 0.6
per cent. In one year, twenty selected mineral corporations, because of these special concessions, were able
to pay taxes at an effective rate of only 19.3 at a time
when other industries in the same income range were
taxed at a 38 per cent rate. First introduced for the
benefit of the small operator faced with the risks
involved in an extractive industry, these depletions
allowances now go primarily to companies with assets
of a million dollars or more. The strange set of tax
loopholes which benefit the mineral lessors in eastern
Kentucky's coal fields has made millionaires of some
strip miners and brought them what *Dun's Review* has
labeled ". . . unbelievably high profits . . ."

The mine operator who does not own land in the
Kentucky mountains must seek out the current owners of the mineral deeds. Then he leases the lands at
a per-ton royalty figure which usually runs twenty-
five cents a ton. The lessor does not need to own
mining equipment or worry about large payrolls. He
can operate out of a clean, air-conditioned office in
some distant city and take the wealth of the hills
without getting coal dust on his hands. One such
lessor operates out of Philadelphia, and one of the
biggest of all is located in London, England.

The mineral-rights owner is permitted to figure

his tax on a capital-gains basis instead of straight income. Then, in addition, he has a cost-depletion allowance working in his favor. This is based on the original cost of the mineral rights.

According to the Kentucky Division of Reclamation, the average yield of coal in its mountain counties is more than 6000 tons per acre. The lessor of mineral rights for that acre, at his twenty-five cents per ton, would be paid $1500. Even though he might be a millionaire in a top-income bracket, he may still have $1200 of it clear after taxes, under the system of special allowances the federal government permits the privileged few in his business. Obviously, these low taxes enable mineral-rights lessors to build huge fortunes on an industry that scars the landscape permanently. In addition to the coal, they have probably already sold timber from the lands. The broad form deed often included the timber use in the original contract. Some mineral-rights owners further sell rights to remove oil and gas from their coal-field lands.

Coal strippers in Kentucky always stand ready to contribute sizable sums, if not directly to a candidate for public office, then to his campaign fund. Then, Edward Breathitt ran for Governor of Kentucky. After visiting the coal fields repeatedly and hearing the stories of people whose homes and work had been destroyed by the strip mine operations, the new governor said, "This is not right," and proceeded to do as much as he could to alter the long-time course of affairs. The strip miners spoke of him thereafter in a language laced with special invectives.

In the following election the candidates for governor were Henry Ward, a member of Breathitt's cabinet, and Louis B. Nunn.

Strip mine operators had no trouble selecting their candidate. They put their money on Nunn. After he reached the governor's chair the strip miners quickly began instructing the state's field inspector from the Department of Reclamation on the facts of political life. One eastern Kentucky miner was reported to have told the inspector from the state Reclamation Department, "We are not taking orders from you. We take our orders from the governor's office. Trouble with you is, you don't know there's been an election."

In spite of the fact that Nunn set the miners straight and went along with Breathitt's hard line, the strip miners attitude and methods pointed up the irrefutable fact that state strip mine laws are effective only as long as they are enforced. This is the overriding weakness in any state strip mine regulation. A change in administration can gut the enforcement machinery, take the heat off the strippers and rippers, and let them go ahead and do largely as they please with the land just as they have historically.

Among those who have given this problem intense study, there is wide agreement that the only answer on the horizon is some form of federal regulation over the strip mining industry. No matter how much we might prefer to see the control rest with the individual states, the fact of life is that the states are incapable of guaranteeing permanent protection to landscapes coveted by the strip miners. The states have repeatedly proved their inadequacy in controlling this industry.

If there is a single secret to effective reclamation of strip mined lands it is, according to Elmore Grim, Kentucky's long-experienced Director of the Department of Reclamation, found in preplanning the removal of the coal and the handling of the overburden. If the topsoil is to go back on top of the reclaimed acreage, it must be set aside as the land is stripped. If highly acid subsoils are to be reburied, this too must be planned in advance. Such preplanning has been consistently resisted by the strippers because it cuts into profits.

In July, 1967, the U. S. Department of the Interior sent its Assistant Secretary of Mineral Resources J. Cordell Moore to Owensboro, Kentucky, where the strip mine industry was conducting a symposium. What Moore told the assembled strip miners was not precisely what they hoped to hear. "I think," he said, "it is evident that federal legislation to deal with the problem of surface-mine damage is on its way. The exact form of such legislation, when it will be enacted, what the scope of its coverage will be, and how it will be administered—are questions that none of us can answer with certainty tonight. But, I feel certain there will be federal legislation eventually."

Six months earlier, Senator Frank J. Lausche, from Ohio, had introduced his S.217. The bill would have authorized the Secretary of the Interior to establish a program within his Department to set up conservation and reclamation policies for strip mined lands, and see that they were enforced. Among the earliest observers to be aware of this newly proposed legislation were the alert mine-industry lobbyists. Senator Lausche was already suspect in their camp. He had long been an open foe of the strip miners methods and their blatant disregard for the welfare of the land. The mining lobbyists were not long swinging into action.

Once hearings were planned for the Lausche bill there were repeated appeals for delays and postponements. The mining industry claimed that it needed time to study the proposal. That the industry needed time was true enough, but it scarcely needed time to "study the proposed legislation." Its provisions were plain enough, especially to the mining industry. On the other hand, delay in hearing a bill can often result in its death which, beyond question, was the aim of lobbyists. The delays came. Hearings were postponed. They were still not underway when Senator Lausche approached the primary elections of May, 1968. To the surprise of many, Senator Lausche was defeated in the primary. While it cannot be said that the mining industry played a role in ending the Senator's long years of tenure in the Senate, that group was surely not grieved by his political demise.

Any time an administration in Washington, or a Congressman, proposes some new bit of legislation that would bring added controls of any kind on the strip mine fraternity, he knows before he starts that he is sticking his hand in a beehive. The watchful mining lobbyists are going to swarm and settle around every area in which they might exert influence against the proposals. Following its report on strip mining in 1967, the Administration of President Lyndon B. Johnson sponsored Senate Bill 3132 which would force miners to do a better job of reclaiming lands stripped in the future. Meanwhile there were in the Senate mill two other similar bills, S.3126 and Senator Lausche's S.217. In addition to dealing with future strip mine scenes, these bills would have tackled the seemingly staggering problem of reclaiming the vast acreages stripped in the past and left by the miners as their gift to future generations.

During 1966, federal government workers totaled the extent of such damage to fish and wildlife habitat by strip mining. There had been 12,898 miles of America's streams damaged. Of our lakes and reservoirs, 145,000 acres had suffered damage from strip miner's digging. And wildlife habitat had been destroyed—more than 1½ million acres of it. Kentucky, alone, had seen 395 miles of its streams seriously polluted by strip mine products, and other states had suffered even more. In Louisiana, surface mining had damaged 1714 miles of streams and 100,000 acres of lakes. Ohio listed 1200 miles of strip mine-damaged streams, and 68,000 acres of wildlife habitat ruined or heavily damaged. *At least thirty-nine states had miles of ruined streams and acres of ravaged land to add to the depressing total.*

The proposed strip mine regulations finally came up for hearings before the Senate Committee on Interior and Insular Affairs and present to speak against them were the mining-interest watchdogs with their familiar refrain. The National Coal Policy Conference claimed that the states were already doing an effective job of regulating strip mining. (As recently as 1964, according to the Department of the Interior report on surface mining, only about a third of the stripped areas were being reclaimed.) Further, said the National Coal Policy Conference, federal legislation would work against the "remarkable progress" being made toward reclamation by the coal companies themselves.

Then a speaker representing the American Mining Congress explained patiently to the Senate committee that, for years already, the coal industry had been doing everything "practicable" to reclaim the lands laid open by its machinery. Of the proposed federal legislation, he said the mining industry wanted to go on record as opposing this ". . . exceedingly heavy-handed approach with grave potential for restricting the healthy development of our industry wholly out of proportion to the size of the problem." Such legislation on the federal level he held to be unnecessary, undesirable, and impracticable.

Someday, someone in the legislative branch of the federal government will eventually steer through Congress the laws to bring the strip miners under federal control. Meanwhile, the brains and money of the strip mine industry are always ready to swing into action opposing any such move. It is, for the miners, a holding action. Change is what they have to fear, because any changes in the laws are almost certain to bring tighter controls over this abuse of the American landscape. It is past time. Citizens offended by this rape of the land can make their beliefs known where it counts. Legislators are sensitive to the opinions of their constituents.

But sadly, federal legislation may make too little difference in the requirements over strip miners in states such as Kentucky where there are already relatively strong strip mine laws. The new federal laws, when they come, may be weaker than the strongest state laws. This is the concensus across the coal fields of America. So the people must be vigilant and see that such federal legislation must be at least as strong as the strongest state law. No state, including Kentucky, West Virginia, and Pennsylvania, is doing all it should to correct the evils inherent in the strip mining process.

Strip mining has no place in the mountains where the land cannot be restored to its original slope. In the less mountainous country where area strip mining is practiced, we can also do much more than we are doing. The land should be put back, not to meet the conditions of some weak law which speaks of "gently rolling topography," or says "where practical," but to its "approximate original contour." The cost is generally believed to be below ten cents per ton of coal mined, although coal companies are careful to keep such reclamation costs top secret.

Even the regions that have been violated by the strip miners, and have since been returned to a semblance of their original contour, may not be free for all time of the shovel's bite. In western Kentucky, the coal companies are holding on to their mined lands. Beneath some of them lie deeper seams of coal that might be reached at some future date. In a single decade the strip miners nave reached steadily deeper into the earth with their giant machines to increase the depth of overburden they can move from around forty feet to one hundred feet. No one is saying how far they can go to reach seams of coal that lie still deeper. The machine manufacturers claim they can construct strip mine shovels of almost any imaginable size, but the next big problem is that the coal seams cannot support the weight of these monsters.

Technological advances can be expected to solve such problems. Much of the land that has been stripped, and perhaps restored outside the mountains, is in danger of being restripped in the years ahead. Meanwhile, in the mountains the growing value of coal will send the operators back to the coal fields to remove those deposits which economics or the lure of the fast buck kept them from taking the first time through. In some instances the coal shovels may be replaced by burning the coal in place beneath the earth and harnessing the energy, thus bypassing the need to remove the coal and haul it away.

Hopefully, the line of opposition to the strip mine machines will continue to stiffen. No one denies the benefits which coal has brought a developing nation and a bustling economy, but if men are to find on this land the necessities of life hundreds of thousands of years from now, we must cure ourselves of the expediency complex. We must look to the land with a deeper understanding, because the land is life and to destroy the land limits life.

12. Just Pass a Law

In the sordid history of surface mining, miners operating on private land have felt no controls except those imposed by their respective states—and the single greatest characteristic of state strip mine legislation has been its woeful inadequacy. Some states have laws stronger than others, and those that do invariably brag about it, as well they might, because it is no small accomplishment forcing regulations upon the wealthy mining industry. But no matter who has the strongest strip mine controls, the fact remains that, to date, no state has exercised enough control over the mining and reclamation activities of its open-pit coal miners.

Not surprisingly, the strip miners disagree. They complain in a loud and public manner that the laws of their respective states are strong, effective, and sometimes punitive.

In recent years more and more concerned citizens have begun to insist that the strip mine industry be brought under better control. Wherever strip mined fields lie barren beneath the sky, men ask themselves what good these lands now are, how they can be put to productive use after both the coal and the men who took it from the earth are gone. Some of the suggestions have been strange indeed.

Late in 1967 the bustling city of Columbus, Ohio, was listening carefully to a plan advanced by the New York Central Railroad which proposed to operate a trash train to haul solid wastes from Columbus to

Perry County, fifty-five miles to the east, and there
dump it into the old coal strip pits. To some, this
scheme from the solid waste-disposal engineers seemed
an ingenious answer to two growing problems. To
others, especially around the Perry County seat town
of New Lexington, the idea was most repugnant. When
emissaries of the New York Central journeyed to New
Lexington for a public meeting, delegations of citizens
walked out and others made angry statements that
they did not care to see their county become the trash
dump for Columbus. There were sharp questions
about whether the garbage would introduce stream
pollution to this largely rural county. The native Perry
Countain was confronted with the fact that his home-
land was being twice defiled. Both strip mining and
garbage dumping seem somehow to be poor ultimate
uses for a land remembered by some as beautiful,
rolling farm country.

This question of solid-waste disposal confronts communities over much of the country. The waste must
come to rest somewhere, preferably out of sight down-
wind from civilization.

Philadelphia, which during 1967 incinerated more
than 800,000 tons of refuse and sent the fumes into
the heavily burdened atmosphere, in 1968 began
sending its garbage on freight cars to the abandoned
coal fields one hundred miles away. Meanwhile, numerous other major cities and counties, including
Westchester County, New York; New Haven, Con-
necticut; Reading, Pennsylvania; Toronto, Canada;
Providence, Rhode Island; and Washington, D.C., had
similar negotiations underway.

In spite of the fact that there is something basically
vulgar about the scheme, it is difficult to deny the
logic of dumping garbage into the abandoned strip
mines. In his efforts to convert the landscape to his
needs, man had already perverted the natural struc-

ture of the earth, when he stripped away the over-burden. Then he replaces the fossil fuels, the product of the ages, with his own garbage. Catlike, he covers the evidence and leaves the scene, unbothered by moral concern about his right to bequeath the future a great garbage sandwich where rich seams of coal had lain. After due thought, garbage and strip mined lands seem somehow to deserve each other. And this proposal demonstrates, as few other developments might, the true worth of lands that have felt the strip miner's bite.

In the "Wonderful World of Ohio," at the same time, there was already underway a project geared to search out exciting new uses for Ohio's 276,700 acres of strip mined land, as well as those acres to be mined in the years ahead. In 1965 the administration of Governor James A. Rhodes contracted with a group of Cleveland consulting engineers, at a cost of $56,500, to suggest what might be done with the state's strip mined lands. In due time, the firm delivered to the Ohio Department of Natural Resources a pair of loose-leaf notebooks totaling about 150 pages, reflecting a search of the literature and an effort to suggest a course of action.

Under the heading of "Opportunities," the firm advanced the startling conclusion that "The study area offers an opportunity to balance Ohio's recreation spectrum through provision of low-density wilderness-type activities. Hunters, hikers, wilderness campers, naturalists, and pleasure drivers seeking unique experiences can be satisfied in the study areas. Due to the broken terrain and isolation of parts of each site, unusual outdoor pursuits such as cycle trails, rifle ranges, and amateur rocket-launch sites not found in other public areas could be accommodated."

The inference was plain that Ohio had, in its 276,700 acres of strip mined lands, a treasure chest for outdoor-minded citizens if they would only change their attitudes and look upon these artificial badlands as a valuable resource.

Among the variety of camps for which the consultants saw hope in the strip mines were "fresh-air camps," "special-interest camps," and "camps for the handicapped." As one Ohioan summed it up, "A beginning camper could go to the strip mines, start out in a fresh-air camp, fall over a high bank, and end up in a camp for the handicapped."

It's all a matter of viewpoint. The writer of recommendations for the state of Ohio chose to see strip mines as a land of opportunity, "The open rugged topography of the strip-mined areas is an asset . . . the visitor is presented a totally fresh environmental experience. Pleasure drivers will find a wealth of scenic change."

What do you do with those unsightly high walls, the artificial crumbling cliffs that face the last open cut in strip mine fields? "High walls can be exploited (sic) as interpretive centers explaining regional geology. Coal tipples, spoil banks, and high walls can be used as educational features explaining the mining process."

It was even hinted that there might be sound reason for not reclaiming all the stripped lands. "Unreclaimed surface-mined areas can be viewed as demonstrations in ecological succession of plant material and wildlife."

In an allied study of the Perry County area, fisheries specialists investigated 139 ponds for such qualities as oxygen content, temperature and vegetation, and found that only eleven were capable of supporting fish life. This was in spite of the fact that the strip mining was done largely *after* the state required reclamation measures under laws that the mining companies have consistently labeled "severe."

Ohio officials looked with favor upon the recommendations for the Perry County area and sought bids on "Phase I," which consisted of grading and reclaiming some 2500 strip-mined acres. According to the consultants estimate, this would cost $390,000, and would get the area ready for "Phase II" which would cost another $390,000. Whatever the eventual expenditures, 75 per cent was to come from federal funds under the Appalachian Regional Development Act.

Ohio, and other states as well, might first devote their efforts to seeking adequate controls over the destructive strip mine industry. The need for day camps in strip mine areas is far less than the need for laws strong enough to prevent adding acreage to these problem lands.

The first state to adopt any legislative controls over its strip mine industry was West Virginia in 1936. By 1967, according to the Department of the Interior publication *Surface Mining and Our Environment,* only nine other states had statutes regulating surface mining. Indiana had followed with a law passed in 1941, Illinois 1943, Pennsylvania 1945, Ohio 1947, Kentucky 1954, Maryland 1955, Virginia 1966 and Tennessee 1967. All of them have certain provisions in common. Strip miners in these states generally have to file applications for permits, and perform a certain amount of grading and reclamation within specified time limits, and post performance bonds.

No state, according to the report, can hope to obtain effective strip mine control without strong laws adequately enforced. And these are obtained and made to work only where there is an informed public and a concerned legislature.

If you were suddenly to be elected governor of a state where the strip mine industry operates, the safest course of action would be to ignore it and hope everyone else did the same. Play it cozy and you might get through a term or two in the statehouse without one of those bloody strip mine battles. You would thereby have adopted the usual course.

The other, and more politically hazardous, approach is sometimes chosen by that rare politician determined to make the strip miners good citizens. Once committed, the chances are that, come hell or acid-mine waste, he must fight the strip mine battle through to its bitter end. Always ready and alert for such a move is the state's strip mining organization, usually bearing a name intended to link it with the forces of conservation, or at least tree planting. This "reclamation" group can bring all manner of pressures to bear on legislators who threaten to tamper with existing laws or make things more restrictive for the strip mine industry.

This was all well known to Kentucky's newly elected Governor Edward T. Breathitt when he announced in 1965 that he would seek to strengthen the state's strip mining regulations. Early in his term he visited one of the state's busiest strip mine fields and stood in the shadow of the giant shovel eating away at his native state. "If they can build a machine that can tear down a mountain," he said, "they can build a machine to put it back." This much, of course, they could not do. It depends on the steepness of the slope as the governor was later to acknowledge. What the governor had determined was that Kentucky coal miners must do a better job of repairing the land they tore up. The strip mining industry realized that this troublesome governor intended to give them a stiff fight. "This is a simple and clear issue," he said, "a struggle between powerful special interests and our children's inheritance."

He foresaw a time when, unless the industry was properly policed, Kentuckians would have to buy up hundreds of thousands of acres of ravished land and restore it at public expense. "I don't think," he stated, "the taxpayer should have to restore the damage the wealthy strip mine operators cause. I think the operators themselves should do it."

At this point Kentucky's Commissioner of Natural Resources J. O. Matlick handed an assignment to Dave Schneider, a youthful attorney in his department. He was to conduct a study of all the strip mine legislation in states that had passed such laws. From these they intended to sift the strongest features, then add a few of their own to come up with a new strip mine law for Kentucky.

When completed, the newly proposed legislation acknowledged the fact that strip mined lands in western Kentucky's rolling terrain present a totally different reclamation problem from the one faced in the mountains of Appalachia. In the west, the mine operators would be required to restore the land to a contour which could be worked by farm machinery. And, unless it could be used to help form a state-approved lake, the steep final cut would have to be reduced to a 45 degree slope by filling.

In the mountains of eastern Kentucky it would be necessary to terrace the slopes and establish waterways. All such areas were to be seeded to vegetation. Important was the stipulation that the miner failing to meet his commitments on reclamation could be put out of business any time by the state.

The anticipated outcries and the flurries of telegrams began to descend on the governor's office in Frankfort. Three identical telegrams came from one miner in Madisonville, a city that had recently appropriated $100,000 for a plane and pilot to spray old strip mine pits where clouds of mosquitoes bred.

In an effort to sell the bill to legislators, the governor organized a flying trip to eastern Pennsylvania where a similar law had been in effect. Sixty Kentuckians made the journey and, not surprisingly, the flight took them at low altitudes across the ravaged mountains in the eastern part of their own state. It was an eye-opening experience for a number of lawmakers and a blow for the strip miners.

Some Kentucky legislators wanted to ask in Pennsylvania about the validity of the old strip miner cry that a new law would put the miners out of business. This was the same outcry heard in the hills of Pennsylvania as that state forced its miners to accept its first strong set of strip mine legislative controls. In a 1965 tabulation, Pennsylvania was found to have 302,400 acres disturbed by strip mining operations, the largest acreage of any state. According to U. S. Department of the Interior calculations in 1967, Pennsylvania strip mines had polluted and damaged 3000 miles of streams, 292,000 acres of wildlife habitat and destroyed 2020 acres of water in four reservoirs. Pennsylvania citizens who had watched the miners dig with unfettered abandon had been unable to slow the assault on the land.

The proposed legislation, then considered the toughest in the country, was introduced in 1961 and, although the coal lobby battled it savagely, the bill finally made it through the lower house. But the strip mine bill still had the barriers of the state senate to hurdle and in these chambers the politicians in behalf of the coal industry managed to decorate the bill with enough amendments to make it almost bearable. Even so, the new Pennsylvania law was widely praised.

Out in the coal fields, however, the mine owners were still predicting disaster. One predicted that the state's new law would put 100,000 Pennsylvanians out of jobs.

The new Pennsylvania law called for a strip mine license fee of $300 per year on each mining operation and stipulated that operators not adhering to the law would be out of business. Operators were placed under a minimum $5000 bond and legally prohibited from polluting streams. They were required to return stripped land to its original contour where the pits were less than one hundred feet deep, and negotiate with the state on reclamation details for deeper cuts. If they failed to obtain a license before opening a mine they could be both fined and jailed.

Were mine operators forced out of business? In 1960 strip mine operations in Pennsylvania produced 28,148,000 tons of coal in all grades. By 1965, with the new and stricter law enforced for several years, the state's coal production had risen to 29,677,000 tons, an increase of one and a half million tons.

Economically, the Pennsylvanians learned that the required reclamation work cost, during the following years, an average of $343 per acre stripped. During legislative hearings Kentucky's strip mine industry had claimed that the proposed law of 1966, if passed, would cost them as much as $6900 per acre. Why would the cost of reclamation in Kentucky be so much higher than the cost of similar work in Pennsylvania? The answer, of course, was that it would not. Testimony of Commissioner Matlick and his Director of Reclamation, Elmore C. Grim, rearranged the quoted figures for those wanting the truth. Calling the $6900 figure, ". . . a purely hypothetical claim of the Kentucky Coal Industry," Grim told the legislators, "They have never spent this amount on a single acre of land in Kentucky. You may wonder why the . . . figure is so out of line with actual Pennsylvania experience. The answer is simple. The Pennsylvania officials stated that the key to reclamation at the lower cost is the careful preplanning of where the overburden is to be placed. The figure cited to you by the Kentucky coal operators assumes that every cubic yard removed to uncover coal must be pushed or carried the maximum total of 390 feet. Of course, any such needless work would inflate the cost estimate. Any time you move the maximum amount of dirt the furthest distance possible," Grim summarized, "you will come up with an astronomical figure."

There was more to the story. Grim then compared the economics of coal stripping in Pennsylvania with the Kentucky coal fields. As any strip miner knows, the profits possible in stripping an area are largely determined by the depth of the overburden and the thickness of the uncovered coal seam, or its yield in tons. Grim explained to Kentucky legislators that Kentucky coal fields were richer than those of Pennsylvania. Official records of the United States Bureau of Mines revealed that the ratio of overburden to coal in Pennsylvania is 14 to 1. But in Kentucky it is 8 to 1. "This means that the Pennsylvania operator must go much deeper and remove almost twice the amount of dirt and overburden per ton of dug coal that the Kentucky operator does. And while the Pennsylvania operator takes an average 3000 tons per stripped acre, his Kentucky counterpart will market as much as 14,000 tons per acre in the rich fields of western Kentucky." If strip miners could make a profit under Pennsylvania conditions, it seemed obvious that the Kentucky operators could stand the cost of reclamation under the newly proposed law. "We honestly believe," Grim told the legislators, "that the additional cost of reclamation under Senate Bill 3 will be somewhere between five and eleven cents per ton in Kentucky." Later figures showed it to be about seven cents per ton.

During the controversy, Kentucky citizens journeyed from the mountains to Frankfort to state their views on strip mining. From the mountain settlement of Honey Gap, in Knott County, came Mrs. Ollie Combs, a frail little widow. When the bulldozers threatened to cover up her home, she threw her body in front of the grinding machine. The incident brought national attention to her plight. Arrested, she spent Thanksgiving Day in the county jail. "Strip mining," she testified "is poisoning the waters and destroying the land." Legislators were so impressed that they applauded her.

Then Mrs. Eda Ritchie from Sassafras Hollow told a hushed legislative assembly of the day a strip miner's bulldozer dug into her little family graveyard. "Me and my husband was sick in bed," she said, "when they plowed my baby's grave out of the ground. I liked to lost my mind. I couldn't find the place because they had tore it all up."

When the voting was completed, the governor's conservation law had passed with a wide margin, and Kentucky, often viewed as backward in years past, had risen to the top of the list among states that have tried to curb their strip mining abuses.

But strip miners had still not heard the last of Governor Breathitt. Only ten days before turning his office over to his successor at the end of his term on January 1, 1968, he imposed on those who operate strip mines in the mountains a new restriction on the steepness of the slope they may attack. Previously they had been able, under law, to mine slopes up to 33 per cent. Now they could strip no slope greater than 28 per cent. They were still permitted to auger slopes up to 33 per cent. Again there was the old outcry, and the prediction that this would put them out of business. If it did, this is perhaps as it should be. But Governor Breathitt noted that within three weeks following passage of the 1966 law, there had been a new announcement by the American Electric Power Company that it was to quadruple the size of its eastern Kentucky plant on the Big Sandy. The cost would be $100 million. And the new plant created a market for two million additional tons of Kentucky coal per year. In the months following passage of the new law, Kentucky granted new strip mining permits on 12,000 acres—double the acreage of the previous year, and granted mining permits on forty-four new operations, ten of them from operators outside Kentucky.

For the Kentucky strip mine lobby there was still a possibility of crippling the state's hard-won new law. Senate Bill 149 was introduced about the time Governor Breathitt was going out of office. This bill would change the composition of the Kentucky Reclamation Commission which interprets the law and establishes policy over the state's strip mine control agency. From three members, including the commissioners of Natural Resources, Reclamation, and Mines and Minerals, it would be enlarged to a six-member commission. The Director of Reclamation would be removed. Onto the new commission, to oversee the state's strip mine industry, would go the commissioners of Agriculture and Commerce, along with two strip mining representatives to be appointed by the governor. Then, the two strip mine representatives could control the board by enlisting the vote of any other member and it was believed that this would not be difficult considering the fact that the Commissioner of Commerce and the Commissioner of Mines are usually more closely allied with industry than with forces of conservation.

Fortunately, Senate Bill 149 received an unfavorable report from the committee that considered it and died for the time being. Conservationists in Kentucky, however, have little doubt that some such tactic will again be attempted. The state legislature meets every two years, and the persistent strip mine industry will find ways to weaken the laws under which it operates if the forces of conservation relax.

As Stewart L. Udall wrote in *Surface Mining and Our Environment:* "This preoccupation with short-term gain too frequently has ignored the long-term social costs involved—the silted streams, the acid-laden waters, the wasteland left by surface mining . . . We are an affluent society; but we can no longer tolerate (or afford) either prodigal waste of natural resources or cumulative degradation of our environment.

"Each generation has only a temporary rendezvous with the land; despite fee titles and documents of ownership we are no more than brief tenants on this planet."

Viewed in these terms, and their logic is undeniable, the continued permissiveness which allows any group to make devastating permanent changes on the landscape becomes inexcusable in a maturing society. The time is long past for calling a halt to strip mining on the mountainsides that cannot be replaced in their original contour.

Increasingly, conservationists have come to understand that federal control over strip mining is justifiable. While we argue the fine points of jurisdiction between state and federal governments, the strip miners continue to drag the mountains down. Those who follow us by a century or more will harvest the scars. We may not put the mountains back, but we should at least bring a halt to those forces destroying them.

PART IV

"The estuary is home to a wondrous collection of terrestrial and aquatic life . . . Nature alters it by storms, tides, and invasions of animals and plants. But man has had by far the larger impact. Nearly everything he has done along the coastline has damaged estuarine areas."

The Third Wave

13. An Ocean View

Our probing, exploring search for wealth has extended our land grabbing all the way to the edge of the continent and into the salt water beyond. Today, we inflict permanent damage on our national productivity by mistreating the estuaries—those cradles of life where the river flows to the sea and the worlds of salt and fresh water mingle in an ever-changing, vibrant, and pulsing community of living creatures. We have too often looked upon these shallow waters as wastelands to be dredged, filled, and degraded with our refuse. In this disregard we have permitted widespread ruin of one of the most productive of all the wild communities we inherited. Even as we awaken to the enormity of our loss, the ruin continues week by week.

On the sandy north shore of Long Island, the town of Brookhaven, New York, owns title to an incredibly fertile and productive harbor and salt marsh which long ago was named Mount Sinai. Nourished by rich organic nutrients accumulated in the bay over the ages, the marsh became, for the people of Brookhaven, a natural refuge close at hand for bird watching, fishing, and clamming.

Though it looked to some of the town fathers like wasteland, too wet to build on and too dry to float a boat, it was in reality incredibly productive. According to a report of the New York Conservation Department, the tidal flats of the harbor had a capitalized value for shellfish alone of more than $5000 per acre. "Within and around the harbor," said the New York Conservation Department in its magazine *The Conservationist,* "lived multitudes of plant and animal life. Here was a nesting area for black ducks and mallards, a rest stop for other migratory waterfowl and a nursery area for flounder, weakfish, and bluefish. Through the dense growths of smooth cord grass and bullrushes prowled herons and clapper rails. The harbor bottom abounded with marine worms, snails, shellfish, and countless micro-organisms. On the barrier beach grew stands of red cedar, beach plums, and prickly pear cactus. Diamondback terrapins paddled through the water, and at low tide the exposed mudflats came to life as small fiddler crabs emerged from their holes and scuttled about looking for food. Around the shoreline lived fox, opossum, meadow mice, mink, muskrat, masked shrew, raccoon, rabbit and whitetail deer. The harbor was a thriving, fertile, productive mass of life."

Beneath these biological riches, however, lay a bed of fine gravel carried there ages ago by ancient streams. Tempted by the easy availability of these building materials, the town of Brookhaven applied to the U. S. Army Corps of Engineers for a permit to dredge in the harbor, and on August 18, 1955, the Corps, which in this case had little choice, issued the permit. For a decade the dredge chewed away at the floor of the Mount Sinai Harbor.

This destruction demonstrated to the people of the area the extent of their loss. When the town applied again in 1966 for another dredging permit, which would have destroyed an additional forty acres of the harbor, the citizens arose and protested. Finally—with 65 per cent of the salt marsh already gone—the destruction was halted.

If you were to study a list of the important commercial fish taken by our fleets every year, you would find that seven of the ten top-producing species rely at some stage of their lives on the shallow and fertile estuaries for their very survival. Likewise, most of the valued sport fish sought by millions of anglers each year depend on the estuaries for either their own welfare or food fish produced there. In these waters with their relatively low concentration of salt, and their wealth of minute food organisms, grow the nation's annual $30 million oyster crop. And, according to the American Littoral Society, the commercial catch of eighteen important species of fish dependent upon the coastal waters diminished by one half in a recent five-year period—1960 to 1065.

In 1958, the University of Texas Bureau of Business Research published a study entitled "Marine Resources of the Corpus Christi Area." The annual value of the estuaries of the Corpus Christi and Aransas bays, as estimated by this study, came to $370 per surface acre. Into this had come calculations of the worth of recreation and sport fishing, commercial fishing, minerals, transportation, and a few lesser benefits. Not all those benefits mentioned are dependent upon the proper balance between salt and fresh waters in the estuary. However, recreation and commercial fisheries—which taken together totaled an estimated $166.25 per acre annually in the Corpus Christi area—could be seriously damaged and perhaps destroyed by permanently and drastically altering the nature of the estuarine waters. And these resources alone, for the 1.3 million acres covered by the study, were computed to have an annual $216 million benefit to the Texas economy.

While wild creatures abound in this dynamic, shallow-water transition zone, man finds the nearby shoreline among the most attractive areas on earth. We have sought out the estuaries where great rivers enter the oceans as sites for our largest cities. Seven of the world's ten largest metropolitan areas—New York, Tokyo, London, Shanghai, Buenos Aires, Osaka, and

Los Angeles—stand on the shores of estuaries. Within the United States 30 per cent of the population lives within fifty miles of the coast. In addition, human populations are concentrated up the valleys of the rivers from which the estuaries receive their fresh-water supplies. This expanding and spreading human force exerts an overpowering pressure on the fragile estuarine complex.

We attack the estuaries from both ends. Historically we seek out the convenience of the river bottoms to build our cities. Then with the river so near, it is convenient to run our wastes into its waters. The river carries the pollutants down to the edge of the sea and there spreads them out in a growing and thickening blanket. Meanwhile, we find more direct methods of assault upon these shallow productive waters. With dredges and pumps and concrete mixers we destroy the estuaries, thus obliterating any possibility that we might, in some future more enlightened time, restore them to their historic role in the world of nature. The ways in which we have attacked and damaged the estuaries, often beyond recovery, are numerous and sometimes imaginative. Most of the damage is simply the by-product of a fast-paced civilization, and our fast-buck economy.

Spreading out across the estuarine waters, there are in addition to great tonnages of wastes from our sewage-disposal plants, vast quantities of chemical materials from our industries, chlorinated hydrocarbons washing down from the insecticide-treated farmlands, the billowing mud and silt carried off the lands we have stripped of its natural vegetation, and sometimes an unnaturally high degree of heat is lent to the waters by atomic-powered or fossil-fueled power plants.

Two hundred million gallons strong, the effluent from sewage-treatment plants serving our nation's capitol feeds into the shallow waters of the upper Potomac estuary daily. In 1964, it was estimated that this adds eight million pounds of phosphorous and 25 million pounds of nitrogen a year to the estuary waters, and it is anticipated that this will nearly double by the year 2000.

We have further modified the nature of the estuaries by controlling the flow of the fresh water that feeds into them. We dam the rivers and divert the waters for irrigation and other purposes. While the foreign materials that we feed into the nation's estuaries may conceivably be stopped and the injury corrected, man's structures which control the flow of the waters are of a more permanent nature. Only in recent times have we begun to fully appreciate the fact that the estuaries themselves need continued supplies of fresh water.

In the subtropics of the Florida peninsula, dikes are fashioned by scraping materials from the shallow tide lands. Then a soupy mixture of solids and salt water is pumped day after day from beyond the dike to the area behind it. The water runs out and as the bottom builds up, man has created dry land where wetlands were before. On this sun-baked foundation rise whole communities of modern homes and businesses including sprawling, costly vacation centers.

Ocean City, a ribbon of homes and businesses a mile or so wide and ten miles long on Maryland's eastern shore, faces two large bays, Wight and Rehoboth, the feeding and nursery grounds for countless shore birds, shellfish, and fin fish. Since 1952, 737 acres of these marshlands have been converted to land-development projects. Recently there have been steeps taken to destroy an additional 1400 acres of the wetlands by filling them in to provide building space for three new housing developments. Already sacrificed permanently, say Maryland's biologists, is almost half of the fish and shellfish population of the two big bays. Likewise, those who understand the importance of the shallow nursery areas for marine fish are concerned about the welfare of the famed white marlin. Ocean City likes to call itself the "white marlin capitol of the world." White marlin may not be found in the shallows, but the menhaden on which they feed depend on the estuaries.

This Maryland development is a classic example of what happens when the control of such vitally important ecological areas are handed to local authorities. In 1965, the Maryland State Legislature created the Worcester County Shoreline Commission. The new commission could authorize developers to dredge and fill along the shoreline. Repeatedly, we hear the cry for return of government to the local level. But where a resource is destructible and non-renewable, we too often see local authorities assign its long-time value scant importance in the search for a broader tax base and increased local income.

During the 1920s the Albemarle and Chesapeake Canal was altered by removal of a guard lock. Into Back Bay and Currituck Sound—a long famous waterfowl area—flowed a new invasion of salt water. For 10 years the salt water intrusion continued before a new lock was finally installed. But the ditching and dredging did not stop, and the sediment from these operations continued to destroy the valued wild foods and threatened the migratory waterfowl along the Atlantic flyway. As pointed out in the U. S. Fish and Wildlife Service Volume, *Waterfowl Tomorrow*, " . . . most of the large marsh area along the Delaware River has been destroyed during the past few centuries."

Since 1717, men choosing to live at the mouth of the mighty Mississippi have attempted to protect themselves from its unruly waters by constructing levees which have now grown as high as thirty-five feet.

Run-off is faster and consequently carries more silt into the big estuary at the mouth of the river flowing into the Gulf of Mexico. The nutrient complex in the estuaries has changed and the salinity has increased and been stabilized. What happens as a consequence to the salt-water creatures that once lived in these estuaries? No one knows all the answers. But marine biologists tell us that species changes are underway; some of the oyster reefs are gone and others will follow.

For seventy miles through the coastal marshes of Louisiana, the Gulf Outlet Channel Project reaches from the Gulf Coast to the shallow, brackish waters of Lake Ponchartrain. Thirty-six feet deep, 500 feet wide at the bottom, this ditch, according to biologists, affects some 2100 square miles of productive coastal marsh important to waterfowl and fur bearers. Hopefully, the structures being built into the ditch will preserve the marshes against the tendency of the deep channel to drain away the life-giving water.

Of all the nation's plans that might be felt in the ecosystems of its estuaries, none is quite so bold and few so potentially destructive as the water-control system that Texans have devised. Unveiled in May of 1966, by its creator, the Texas Water Development Board, the Texas Water Plan was to cost billions, and permit no drop of water to escape to the Gulf Coast estuaries without the blessings of the state of Texas. Why did Texas need a water plan? As Joe G. Moore, Jr., then Chairman of the Texas Water Development Board, explained before a convention of the American Society of Civil Engineers in 1967, there were already enough water plans of varying dates of origin to "pave a four-lane highway from Texarkana to El Paso." But, Moore added that Texans were seeking more productive use of the 40 million acre-feet of water that flowed across the state's surface every year, as well as those acre-feet which might be recovered from beneath its surface. "You can see the way the rivers flow," he said, "southeastward to the Gulf. You can see the man-made reservoirs which already exist. What then creates the problem? The Houstons, the Dallases, the Fort Worths, the Lubbocks, the San Angelos, the El Pasos, the Amarillos, the San Antonios, the Corpus Christis— people. The distribution of our water supply doesn't match the distribution of our people and their needs— and this maldistribution will be aggravated as time passes. . . . What happens when the supply is exhausted?" The Texas water plan was to reassure the people that the supply might not be exhausted—that there might be adequate water for all their uses through and beyond the year 2010. Included in the comprehensive proposal were 53 new reservoirs, additional work on six that already existed, and construction of half a dozen salt-water barriers—all part of a vast water-redistribution system, 980 miles long from northeast Texas to the southwestern part of the state.

Even by harnessing all its waters in a vast spider web of canals stretched across the face of the state, there would still be less water than the Texans wanted. So to supplement what they have available within their state, they have studied the possibilities of ditching in 16 million feet of water annually from the Mississippi River. Into this great and comprehensive plan was poured the combined thinking of commissions and councils, industries and institutions of higher learning, the Corps of Engineers and the Bureau of Reclamation.

The total cost, said Director Moore, if Texas finished the project as now planned, would be in excess of six billion dollars. Some of the waters thus controlled would—the Texas water board finally assured the commercial fishermen and the marine biologists—be permitted to escape into the complex of estuaries that lie in the Texas Gulf Coast. But just how much fresh water might be needed to maintain this estuarine life, and at what intervals, and in what quantities it should be released, has never been fully understood by marine biologists and much less by the engineers. If the estuaries of this portion of the coast are to be preserved and their biological values retained, the first step is to mount the best available research effort. The wealth of the estuaries and the marine ecosystems dependent upon them call for nothing less.

But if the estuaries of Texas face a massive threat from the water-control structures upstream, they face a more direct and destructive force in a group of mammoth machines clawing up mud and oyster shell in the shallow waters of the bays. A powerful coastal industry is based on this dredging of oyster shell. Even before the birth of the automobile, horse-drawn scoops and farm wagons moved shell from the beaches to the nearby villages to patch up holes in sidewalks and streets. With the passage of time, man's needs for the shell increased and his equipment for recovering it improved. In 1905, the first mechanical dredge moved onto the shallow waters of a Texas bay. In 1912, the first hydraulic dredge went into service there. Since that time the shell industry has grown, both in volume production and in political muscle. From a production of five million cubic yards of shell annually at the end of World War II, the Texas dredgers by 1968 were extracting some eleven million cubic yards of shell from the rapidly dwindling oyster beds.

This is performed by a handful of companies operating a fleet of massive dredging machines, feeding a steady line of shell, twenty-four hours a day, seven days a week, into a whole flotilla of barges. The barges carry the shell to industrial plants which manufacture cement and other products or use it, as does the Dow Chemical Plant at Freeport, in its process for removing manganese from sea water. But one of the major uses of all—and one which many Texans are least able to justify—is still, as it was decades ago, the maintenance of the state's highways. Fully one-third of the oyster shells dredged from the estuaries in this destructive practice go into highway construction. It is also used for building construction, and manufacture of steel, paper, aluminum, and magnesium.

The dredges that extract the shell suck it up, mud and all, from depths as great as forty feet. Then the mudshell is washed, and, while the shell moves into the waiting barges, the muddy water is flushed back into the bay. It spreads out around the operating dredge in a broad, dark plume of sediment floating like a cloud over whatever remains of the marine community. Large particles such as sand may settle out rapidly. Finer materials may remain in suspension for an interminable time. And the longer it is suspended, the greater are the possibilities that the tides and currents will transport it out over beds of live oysters and other marine creatures which cannot escape it.

Settling sediment can kill oyster beds. This is one way in which the dredges damage the marine environment. More directly, they destroy the oyster-shell beds. To survive, a young oyster must attach itself to a hard surface. Most commonly, under natural conditions, this would be a bed made of the shells of its ancestors. Where it can find nothing but mud, the young oyster perishes. Behind the dredges, more often than not, only mud bottoms exist. There is an ecological relationship between the welfare of the oyster and the vitality of the area as a producer of other organisms. "It should be remembered," said Joe G. Moore, Jr., "that live oyster reefs are an important part of the ecology of the estuary . . . when the bay is good for oysters it is also good for fin fish, shrimp, and crabs."

Strangely enough the state government of Texas is

fostering this destructive dredging of its bays. Before it is permitted to put its dredge to work in an area, a shell company must apply to the State Department of Parks and Wildlife for a permit. Within a few weeks the permit is granted and the dredger goes to work. For every cubic yard of shell that he produces, he pays a royalty to the Department of Parks and Wildlife, either fifteen cents per cubic yard for large shell, or thirteen cents per cubic yard for the finer material. This is generally considered—except by the dredging companies themselves—to be too little for the raw materials taken. Maryland dredgers pay ninety cents per cubic yard. Even at the lower rate, the state of Texas receives about one and a third million dollars annually from the sale of its shell. However, the royalty paid for that portion of the shell which goes to the construction of highways, feeds back, not to parks and wildlife, but to the Texas Highway Department, or the county treasury of those areas where the shell is used. Consequently, a whole network of state agencies embracing fish, wildlife, and highway workers lean on the shell producers for part of their annual income.

To the dredgers, shell is shell, and the question of whether it is taken from a live, producing reef, or an old deposit of fossil shell is unimportant, except economically. It has long been the function of the state's wildlife agency to administer the laws and make many of the rules controlling the dredging of mudshell from its bays. Prior to the election of Governor John Connally in 1962, the rule had been that no dredger was permitted to operate closer than 1500 feet to a live oyster bed, and then only where the shell bed was covered by at least two feet of mud, leaving little doubt that it was, indeed, a "dead" reef. Texas law defines a live oyster reef as one yielding at least five barrels of oysters per 2500 square feet of reef. The Director of the Department of Game and Fish was

Howard Dodgen, an able, long-time administrator in the field of natural resources. Dodgen's research had determined that the average distance from an active shell dredge at which the oyster reefs were safe from being smothered in silt was 1200 feet. The added 300 feet had been a safety factor.

But with the passage of time and the insatiable appetite of the dredges, the reefs vanished and the reserves of shell shrank. The shell dredgers sought repeatedly to move in closer to the reefs than the stipulated 1500 feet. Each time they made application, however, they were rebuffed. Then came the election.

During his campaign John Connally promised the people of Texas that, in the interest of efficiency, he would combine the Department of Parks and the Department of Game and Fish into a single state agency. To this Dodgen saw no major objection, providing the money collected from the sale of hunting and fishing licenses and other sources supporting the Department of Game and Fish not be channeled from it into the ailing Department of Parks. Connally promised that the sources of revenue to Game and Fish would continue going to that branch of the new department. He also implied that he anticipated having Dodgen as head of the new department.

It may well be that Connally did not yet realize that powerful economic interests would bring great pressures for a change in the shell-dredging regulations, pressures to which he would have to yield. The first step was a classic tactic in ridding state government of men considered by political office holders to be undesirable. Suddenly Governor Connally no longer consulted with Howard Dodgen, or any longer spoke with him at all—in spite of the fact that they had been personal acquaintances for many years. Soon the state legislature did as the new governor had requested; it abolished both the old Parks Department and the Department of Game and Fish, creating in their stead a new Texas Department of Parks and Wildlife. In place of the six commissioners who had established policy on parks previously and the nine who had guided the activities of the Game and Fish Department, there were now to be only three. And the governor would be able to appoint all of them at one time. Chosen to fill these commissioners roles was an engineer, Will Odum; James M. Dellinger, a Corpus Christi contractor and one of the major road builders in Texas; and A. W. Moursund, neighbor, close personal friend, and business adviser to the then Vice-President Lyndon B. Johnson.

Almost immediately Howard Dodgen was out of a job. He was notified by the commission that he was being retired, but, for the remaining months until he reached his legal retirement age, was to be retained in the position of adviser. He was further informed that he was not expected to advise, nor was his presence desired in the offices. This done, the new commission set about mollifying the shell dredgers.

Four dredging companies had recently applied for permits to remove shell from all of the protected areas in the Galveston and Trinity bays in the Houston area. They were later to request similar unrestricted permission for the rest of the Texas coast. The new commission and its executive director, Weldon Watson, an administrator who had been imported from the State Welfare Department to head the new Department of Parks and Wildlife, decided that, instead of granting the permission outright, they should hold a public hearing. In spite of the fact that testimony at the public hearing was heavily stacked in favor of the dredgers (their paid expert marine biologist consultant was heard but the state's own marine biologists were not heard) the commission decided that it should still retain some limitations on the dredgers. The dredgers, however, should have found slight reason for complaining. From 1500 feet they were now permitted to work within 300 feet of live oyster reefs. In addition to reducing the limitation to 300 feet, the commission declared that it was no longer necessary to limit shell dredging to those reefs covered by two feet of sediment.

This opened vast new stores of shell for the dredgers. It also gave them an opportunity, as U. S. Congressman Robert D. Eckhardt, a long-time conservation worker and foe of the shell dredgers, explained, to spot a dredge on either side of a reef, work it on both the incoming and outgoing tide, and in this manner smother the reef with sediment. Once dead from the sediment, the reef could then be legally taken.

On reefs not mentioned by name in the new order, the dredgers could operate, providing they met the state stipulation of first moving the live oysters to new beds of shell which they would prepare. This practice had once been limited to small reefs of under ten acres, called "towhead reefs." Even with this new source of shell in the Galveston Bay and Trinity Bay areas, in five years the dredgers had worked out their reserves and were looking around for other bays into which they could move their monstrous shell-eating machines.

Next they turned to San Antonio Bay whose western shoreline is the boundary of the famed Aransas National Wildlife Refuge—the world's only remaining wintering grounds for the long-endangered whooping crane. Five years had passed since I visited Aransas Refuge on the Blackjack Peninsula. Glad for an excuse to return to that highly productive wildlife haven, I went back one autumn just ahead of the whooping cranes to see what the dredgers were doing offshore.

Through the refuge on the narrow two-lane road, I drove back to Mustang Lake. Towering above one end of this lake and above the tops of the live oak trees is a sturdy observation tower built for bird watchers. From this platform watchers may see, during much of every winter, the same family of whooping cranes. They live on the shores of Mustang Lake which is actually a shallow salt-water bay. They feed here in the shallows, along the Intercoastal Waterway, and sometimes across the bay on the edge of Matagorda Island. The tower and the lake looked no different. But turning a few degrees to my left, I could see beyond the edge of the refuge, squatting in the shallow waters of San Antonio bay, a little flotilla of working dredges which had not been there before.

Previously, I had studied the map of the bay. The state had divided it into segments for the convenience of the dredging industry and its own forces collecting royalty from the shell. The dredging companies now had obtained state permission to remove the shell from almost the entire bay. Their permits extended to the very edge of the dry land of Aransas National Wildlife Refuge. In those shallow productive waters along the shores of the bay, feeding grounds of the whooping crane, roseate spoonbill, ibis, and other water birds, the dredges could now move and change the whole bottom structure of the bay. They needed, as well, the permission of the Corps of Engineers because these were considered navigable waters where the Corps has jurisdiction. Already they had obtained their Corps' authorization to dredge the bay bottom almost to the very edge of the refuge.

Dredging such as this can change the whole character of an estuary. When reef is removed, the direction of the flow is often changed. In San Antonio Bay, particularly, the bottom is of very fine materials which, once stirred up by the dredges, tend to remain in colloidal suspension for long periods of time, carried around the bay on the currents and waves before they settle. I flew one afternoon at low altitude over the working barges to see this mud soup rushing out of the great drain pipes that carry the wash waters off the edge of the dredges. It fanned out in dark clouds over the dredged area. Although a living oyster can hermetically seal its shell against the invasion of such foreign materials for periods up to three weeks, a layer of clay or silt settling on it eventually smothers the organism and leaves no secure anchoring base for the spat which would start a new generation.

By moving in on the wintering grounds of the whooping crane, the shell dredgers demonstrated a gross disregard for anything that interferes with their economic aims. For decades, people across both the United States and Canada have been concerned about the threat to the endangered whooping cranes. We have followed the progress of the big birds northward in the spring to their distant nesting grounds in the Wood Buffalo National Refuge, and southward again in the fall to the shores of Texas. We have counted and recounted them, and warned against the threats that stalk them. At great expense the governments of both countries have protected the whooping cranes with their money and scientific efforts.

Then with shocking suddenness comes this new threat, not preceded by biological research which might tell us that the dredges damage or do not damage the whooping crane's chances for survival. While conservationists pondered what course to take, the shell-dredging machines continued their unending destruction of the bay bottoms.

With recognition of the vital importance of the estuaries, there has been a corresponding effort to bring protection. One step in that effort occurred in 1967 when the Corps of Engineers and the Department of the Interior signed a letter of agreement to bring the interest of both groups into consideration of applications for dredging in navigable waters along the seashores. It called upon the Corps to consider the viewpoint of the Department of the Interior as to whether or not the intended dredging or filling would have adverse effect on fish and wildlife resources. But the agreement did not carry the authority of legislation, and while the two government agencies might in time co-operate to make the plan work, its legal weakness was soon seen by the dredgers' lawyers.

To Congressman Bob Eckhardt there was only one source of relief for the remaining shell reefs. "Federal action," he said, "must be taken to save what remains, so that future generations may benefit from a natural resource which took eons to build and which the dredgers may well have destroyed in a few more months."

Bob Eckhardt's next effort was to strengthen the legal machinery by having an amendment attached to the old Rivers and Harbors Act of 1899. It would require the Corps to consider damage that such dredging might render the wildlife habitat. It is a sad fact that by the time such legislation is established, it will already be too late in many estuaries.

What is happening to the estuaries—whether in Texas, Florida, Maryland or on the Pacific Coast—is not alone a state problem. The exploiters would have us embrace the theory that these are matters for local resolution. But the nation's estuaries, in spite of their pollutants, are still national treasures.

These are the places by the edge of the ocean where

marine life begins, treasure chests in the world of nature. But the pirates stalk the treasure and leave the cupboard bare. Time is short. Unless we can find a way to rescue them from dredging and filling, and from additional pollution—the estuaries will vanish as living wild communities.

PART V

14. Cures

We know we can scoop off the mountaintop, hold back the river that flows, drain the wetland, pave the scenic gorge with concrete and bridge the chasm. Our advanced technology has granted us this freedom of choice. Surrounded by our sophisticated earth movers, blasting powders, and giant drills, we are overwhelmed by our own cleverness. "It is," as David Brower of the Sierra Club once told a committee of Congress, "out of public concern that man's ability to control tools should catch up with his ability to fashion them, that the conservation movement has grown." Everywhere around us the scene offers abundant evidence that we have let our tools get out of hand, and to the extent that people are the enemy of their land, they are also the enemy of their descendants—their own species.

At the beginning of the century the world held 1.5 billion people. That figure has more than doubled. This rise in population was documented strikingly in an annual report from the Department of the Interior. "It took all this accumulated time on earth," says *The Population Challenge*, "for man to reach an estimated one quarter billion at the time of Christ. By 1830 that figure had quadrupled to 1 billion. Only 100 years later the 2 billion mark was passed and in the next thirty-five years we had reached 3 billion. Incredibly, the fourth billion will be with us by 1980 and by the year 2000, 6 billion persons may be contending for their place on earth."

Within the United States the population is expected to more than double from its 1965 level of 195 million by the year 2010, when a large percentage of those living here today will still be alive. "As the population grows, the competitors multiply," said Dr. Stanley A. Cain, assistant secretary of the Department of the Interior, to employees of the Branch of Wildlife Refuges in 1967. "We have already lost more battles than I care to remember in trying to fend off highway builders, dam projects, power line rights-of-way, bridge projects, and other developments whose sponsors, often as not, are convinced they are serving the greater public good in wresting land away from the conservation usage, even feeling that they are the real conservationists, in some cases."

At least in part, our new dams are justified by what is viewed as a growing demand for recreation for this exploding population. But the old cry that a new lake will provide some recreation becomes an empty refrain as valleys are flooded and all assume a sameness. Attempting to pack the maximum number of human pleasure seekers into each acre defeats the purpose. Not all people seek the same recreational outlets. There is still a need for variety in the landscape. What we owe our land and ourselves is better planning. Across the face of America there has been too much myopic development, project by project. It is further evident that the individual construction agencies arc not capable of long-range comprehensive planning for the common good. There is something frightening about various government agencies looking out, each for itself, with little concern for the over-all effects of their total assault on the landscape. Increasingly, we must understand that it is not our mission as a species to seek out the remaining corners of the world yet unpaved and undammed with a view to inflicting our handicraft upon them simply because they remain "unimproved."

"We have only lately, and with something of a

shock," Dr. Cain told a Seminar on Environmental Arts and Science at Aspen, Colorado, "come to realize that the way we have approached the world has produced benefits, certainly, but also very unfavorable consequences which we still think of as side effects. What technology has been doing that we now find we don't like, is not the cause of our problems but a symptom of them. The problem is that we have viewed the world mechanically. This is a failure of society, not of science and technology. Take autos, for example. They seem to have become an end in themselves, for the great companies and for the individual man. That, as a result of autos, the air is polluted and roads are often in the wrong place is what we have permitted— not an inevitable consequence of autos *per se*."

Largely, the landscape mistakes are there because we have permitted each agency to go its own way, lay its own plans, pursue its own aims. There have, in recent times, been minor bows taken in the direction of co-ordinating activities of the more than three dozen agencies dealing in problems of water management. Committees are formed and agreements reached. Meanwhile, the agencies continue to pursue their own aims and strengthen their own positions. Agreements between agencies are sometimes palliatives to stave off the threatened passage of a more restrictive law or to help maintain the level of a budget.

Sensitive to changing opinion and trends, the Corps of Engineers keeps its finger to the wind. It does not fight new trends, surely not openly; it joins them. Often, in this manner, it ends up in a position of leadership. It has utilized this technique to assure itself a position of strength in recent efforts to bring co-ordinated treatment into the water management picture.

By 1966 the Corps was deeply involved in at least five regional studies on major watershed-development plans. Looking ahead to 1970 when the federal government expected to have eighteen such regional plans at work, the Corps was already in the position of chairman of three, the Ohio, the Upper Mississippi, and the North Atlantic regions.

There had once been efforts to establish a watershed-conservancy district for the sprawling Missouri River Basin which covers half a million square miles from near St. Louis northwestward into Montana, but these efforts were successfully held off by political forces choosing instead to rely on the Corps of Engineers. Then in 1953, the Corps issued invitations to the governors of the ten states within the Basin asking each to appoint his chief water resource engineer to a Co-ordinating Committee. Next the Corps invited the Fish and Wildlife Service, Department of Agriculture, Bureau of Reclamation, Federal Power Commission, Public Health Service, Geological Survey, and the Weather Bureau to send their representatives. This Co-ordinating Committee has since met twice a year and sometimes more. At the first meeting the representative from the Corps of Engineers was designated as *permanent* chairman.

To strengthen its image as a watershed-planning agency the Corps created additional staff field positions within its Civil Works divisional offices. Included in each section were four new branches. One is known as Environmental Resource Planning with its specialists in ecology, beautification, and recreation. Another deals with "policy and long-range planning," and its duty is to keep Corps people well informed of all the changes in national policy which might affect Corps projects. Then there were new sections dealing with economics and with creating plans.

No one can argue against the need for over-all, basin-wide planning. We have gone too far without it. But the Corps, willing or not, seems hardly the government agency to entrust with the role of regional planner. Just as basic as which valley to flood next, is which valleys not to flood at all, a difficult concept for builders to grasp.

Someone other than the dam builders must determine whether or not the proposed concrete structure is worth more than the broad fertile valley where waterfowl nest, or endangered animals stand against threatened extinction. Highway engineers are not ecologists or objective judges of whether a new road is worth more to the future of the state or nation than the memorial forest or wild park it obliterates. The miners themselves must not be left to determine whether the value of coal really justifies etching the face of America with those long yellow scars.

What can we do to slow this assault against the American landscape? How can we stop the permanent loss of our limited acreage? Obviously, it is not enough to fight piecemeal, rearguard actions, against the polished, full-time professional promoters.

The real basic need is for a number of changes in the canopy of the legislative protection under which the builders and diggers labor. But this need, to which we shall return momentarily, does not rule out the more immediate urgency for an increased public awareness of the ever-present threats. Local, regional, and national conservationist organizations are effective in gathering information and marshaling opposition. In the end, however, the restraint on forces endangering the landscape will come from the influence citizens can exert over state governors and members of Congress. It should not be forgotten that the Corps of Engineers carries out the will of Congress. It also avoids projects which do not have the approval of the governor of the state in which they are located, or waits until there is a change in governors.

Often the fight with the determined builders and diggers leaves only a bitter taste—plus a new dam or highway—but the voice of an individual can sometimes save a natural wonder.

Nineteen miles southwest of Corbin, Kentucky, the waters of the Cumberland River flow down to the lip of a 60-foot limestone cliff, then tumble over in a cascading waterfall that attracts about a million tourists a year. Long ago, visitors to this spectacular falls noticed a strange phenomenon that occurs there on clear nights under a full moon; the moonlight reflected in the falling waters of Cumberland Falls creates a moonbow, one of only two in the world. In 1928 a group of private developers created a fantastic scheme to utilize Cumberland Falls for generation of electric power. It was the kind of wild-eyed idea that attracted great sums of risk capital from the sale of stocks in those booming days just ahead of the Great Depression.

As the developers envisioned their plan, an upstream reservoir would store water to be sent through a tunnel nineteen feet in diameter, and around the falls for delivery to a power plant about a mile downstream. Cumberland Falls would be turned off. Nearby, in the county seat of Corbin, a businessman and life-long community resident, Robert Blair, began organizing local opposition. Citizens around Corbin, under Blair's leadership, formed the Cumberland Falls Preservation Association, Incorporated. They attracted the attention of financier T. Coleman duPont, who purchased the Cumberland Falls outright for $400,000, then handed it over to the Commonwealth of Kentucky to be maintained permanently as a State Park. Part of the deed, although it hardly seemed necessary at the time, read, "provided . . . Cumberland Falls shall be preserved in its existing state . . . and that said property shall not be used . . . for the production of hydroelectric energy."

Over the following years Kentucky added more than $4,000,000 worth of improvements to the Cumberland Falls State Park and the area became one of the most popular attractions in the mid-South. With its work apparently finished for all time, the Cumberland Falls Preservation Association, Incorporated, disbanded.

Then during the 1950s, the ghost of the original scheme suddenly rose again on the banks of the Cumberland. From Williamsburg, Kentucky, Eugene Siler, Jr. had been elected to represent his district in the United States Congress. Siler set the Corps of Engineers to studying all over again the old plan to run the river around Cumberland Falls. The Corps added a few refinements, including enlarging the nineteen-foot tunnel to thirty feet, and building a second dam up Jellico Creek, so the waters for the power plant could be supplemented by the costly pump-storage type system. The cost of the complex, as the Corps anticipated it, came to about $127,000,000 —second only to the Barkley Dam among Kentucky's multitude of public water management projects.

Out of his corner once again came the fiery Bob Blair to reactivate the Preservation Association. He enlisted the aid of others, both locally and throughout the state. An important ally back in the 1928 fight had been Herndon J. Evans of The Lexington *Herald*, and he and Blair enlisted the support of the powerful Louisville *Courier-Journal*. At a public hearing conducted in Corbin by the Corps of Engineers on April 14, 1964, tempers were running high. The ranks of those in favor were heavy with local businessmen who had visions of sudden community wealth. As one of these neighbors of Blair phrased it, speaking of the two dams, power plant and giant tunnel beneath the mountain, "The people want them, the Army Corps of Engineers wants to build them, if built the federal government will pay for them—a modest figure. . . ."

Gaining eloquence the same advocate composed for The Corbin *Daily Tribune*, as message that should have put Blair in his place. "Who would be callous enough," he asked, "to deny the people of Whitley and McCreary Counties . . . their birthright? . . . Yes, how could any informed native son oppose such a God-sent project as this proposes to be?"

But Blair forged ahead in his fight against the proposed gigantic expenditure. At the Corps hearing he produced a copy of the plan proposed in 1928, and also one now proposed by the Corps. Two things were obvious. The new plan was essentially the old plan. And the power plant complex would be right in the heart of the Cumberland State Park which the state was obligated to keep free of such developments. The federal government, however, had never signed a pledge against such development.

The Corps' representative from the Nashville District Office explained that diverting the water would not damage the Falls because they would permit 100 cubic feet per second to flow over it the year around. To Blair, and others working with him, the manipulated natural wonder was repugnant. Who would come to view a falls where the water was turned off and on? The Louisville *Courier-Journal* wondered editorially if the flow might be operated on a coin-machine basiss, so that a half dollar dropped in a slot would let water flow over the falls for a few minutes.

Through this controversy the Corps stood patiently ready to reason with everyone. It had made its study, presented it findings, and requested funds to go ahead with the plan. The "scenic effectiveness" of the falls, their report said, "would be enhanced." The immediate question arises as to what constitutes an engineer's definition of "scenic effectiveness."

Simply by raising the objections, however, Bob Blair and other opponents of the scheme had threatened it. Harmony between state and federal governments is important if such a project is to succeed. Said Senator John Sherman Cooper of Kentucky, "The fact that the project is controversial will have an adverse effect on its passage." By making the plan so obviously controversial, Bob Blair and others of like thinking may well have saved Cumberland Falls, at least for the present.

In April, 1968, the Corps' District Engineer in Nashville notified Kentucky's governor that the Corps had dropped its scheme for the Cumberland Falls project. But friends of Cumberland Falls should take notice of the fact that the project was simply placed on the "inactive" list.

Those who doubt that citizen's groups can save wild lands should also talk with Tom King of the West Virginia Highlands Conservancy. King, a dentist, led this group of conservationists against the road builders who wanted to push a new highway along the ridge of the Allegheny Mountains through one of the most scenic sections of wilderness remaining in the eastern half of the country. Those fighting to keep the Highland Scenic Highway out of this wilderness stronghold, marshaled facts, selected an alternate route, then went to work convincing the governor, Bureau of Public Roads, State Highway Department, and congressional representatives. From the beginning they were told that their case was hopeless. The highway forces were said to be too strong. The route was already chosen and money had been spent on preliminary design for the road where it would penetrate the Spruce Knob area.

The Highlands Conservancy did succeed in obtaining a change in the routing. The proposed thirty miles through the roadless area was moved thirty miles to the west. The Highlands Conservancy obtained support from the Wilderness Society and other groups, but as Tom King explained to me, "This sort of campaign must be conducted by people who reside in the state where the highway is located. Politicians listen more carefully to their own voters."

Such victories may be only temporary. Time passes and those who fought the good fight, pass as well. And in some future year the builders uncover the dusty plan for a dam or highway—and once again extol its virtues. A Corps representative invited to speak before a meeting of the Kiwanis Club in Corbin, told those assembled that as long as the state is not for the project at Cumberland Falls, it would not be built, ". . . even if it remains on the shelf for 1000 years." As long as it is on the shelf—even if it is 1000 years—the Bob Blairs will have to guard against its resurrection.

More permanent solutions must come from the halls of Congress. Although the ranks of the Congressmen are overbalanced by those eager to feed at the pork barrel there are usually a few pioneering public servants who view the diggers and builders objectively, and would like to institute legislation to bring better control to these extravagant programs in water resource management. In his SB 886, Senator Frank E. Moss, of Utah, proposed that the 90th Congress rename the Department of the Interior, The Department of Natural Resources. In this age this would more nearly describe its sphere of responsibilities. But more was suggested than a simple change of name. From the Department of Agriculture, the new department would obtain responsibility for the U. S. Forest Service, as well as some of the watershed work performed by the Soil Conservation Service. From Health, Education, and Welfare would come the government work that department performs in the fields of air pollution and solid-waste disposal. The Navy would hand over to the new Department its Oceanographic Data Center. And the Department of the Army would deliver the cherished Civil Works Function of its Corps of Engineers to the new Department of Natural Resources.

It was not entirely a fresh idea and Senator Moss claimed no credit for its origin. In 1938 Secretary of the Interior Harold Ickes had suggested changing the name of his department to the Department of Conservation. A decade later the Hoover Commission followed with a repetition of the idea. President Eisenhower also made the suggestion that the civil works of the Corps of Engineers be taken over by Interior.

Explaining the need for his proposed legislation, Senator Moss mentioned the strange stop-gap role into which the Bureau of the Budget has evolved. "It is instructive to note," he said, "that the Bureau of the Budget—which was never assigned water-policy functions by Congress—has assumed more and more control on the grounds of fiscal policy. Because no national planning agency exists, and because of the vacuum of responsibility in this field, Budget has become an unofficial planning agency which finds its influence constantly expanding."

One after the other, agencies threatened with loss of parts of their power structure under Senator Moss's proposed change, trooped to the Hill to tell the Senate Committee conducting hearings why their own bureaus should be deleted from the plan. Agriculture wanted to keep Forestry. The Navy wanted to hang on to Oceanography. And, of course, the generals came. General Harold K. Johnson, Army Chief of staff, appeared to plead the Army's case for retention of the Corps' civil works functions. Among the arguments was a familiar one; "If civil works responsibilities are taken from the Army, the technical quality of our personnel and the capability of our Army units would be reduced."

Clearly, the implication is that by maintaining a vast Civil Works Program we are somehow helping to keep our defenses up. But the fact is that most of the Civil Works Program is performed by civilians. At any given moment in peacetime, the Civil Works Program has two hundred or fewer Army officers supervising the work of some 40,000 civilians. That the officers gain experience cannot be denied, but the small number of officers involved lends doubt to the argument that this is an economical training ground for military assignments. Neither has it been fully explained how a colonel, supervising from his Louisville office, the construction of a dam on the Red River in Kentucky is gaining combat experience except perhaps in skirmishes with the conservation forces. If this confrontation constitutes battle experience, the commanding general of the Corps might, for the sake of public relations, be well advised to cease referring to opponents of the dam building mania as "little old ladies in tennis shoes."

Actually, the Corps might as well have relaxed. It is futile speculation to think that Congress—lacking great public pressure—would bring the Corps of Engineers under any authority except its own. Leaders in government agencies are well aware that our hodgepodge of water programs should come under some systematic method of planning for the over-all national good. As it is done today, there is no sound system of priorities. The community whose senator or representative squeaks the loudest gets the grease.

Perhaps the closest we have come to true regional planning was in the creation of TVA which was given broad powers and responsibility by Congress. TVA, permitted to do its own planning has become increasingly concerned in recent years with its own perpetuation, and shown little inclination to stop building even though the job is done.

Created in 1933, the Tennessee Valley Authority worked to control devastating floods, and bring the valley river transportation, inexpensive electric power, and low-cost fertilizer. At the age of twenty, TVA underwent a change in character. The production of electric power became its paramount interest and TVA became the country's biggest customer for strip mined coal. In 1967 it gained congressional approval to begin work on a new dam on the Little Tennessee River. The dam was opposed by many organizations including such groups as the American Forestry Association, National Audubon Society, Trout Unlimited, Tennessee Game and Fish Commission, Tennessee Conservation League, Tennessee Outdoor Writers Association, Tennessee Farm Bureau Association, Tennessee Livestock Association, Southeastern Outdoor Writers Association, Association for Preservation of the Little Tennessee River, the Eastern Band of Cherokee Indians, Fort Louden Association, Greenback Farmers Co-operative, Vonore Lions Club, Chattanooga YMCA, East Tennessee Historical Association, East Tennessee Duck Hunters Association, Sweetwater Valley Feeder Pig Association, Knox County Young Republican Club, and the Middle Tennesse Conservancy Council, among others.

In the Little Tennessee and its tributaries flowing down out of the mountain country of North Carolina and Georgia there were already seven dams. The lower thirty-four miles of the river, however, still flowed free and this was the section TVA wanted to impound with its Tellico Dam. The Southern Industrial Development Council called on the University of

Oklahoma Industrial Development Institute to study the best potential uses of the river. The finding was that the Little Tennessee promised greater ultimate returns if left wild and free-flowing.

Was the reservoir needed for recreation? Within a fifty-mile radius there were twenty-two other dams and reservoirs. So many dams had been constructed throughout the southeast by TVA and the Corps of Engineers that according to the Tennessee Game and Fish Commission, explaining a steadily decreasing sale of non-resident fishing licenses, ". . . impoundments no longer provide the attraction they once did to non-residents."

Why then did TVA insist on the $41,000,000 dam, flooding 14,400 acres? The answer lay in the fact that TVA was moving into the real estate business. The major purpose in creating this reservoir on the Little Tennessee would be to sell land to the industries needing cheap water transportation.

When it was pointed out that the new dam would flood good industrial sites already available in the river bottomland, TVA chose not to hear. Neither did it place importance on a report of the State Local Waterfront Industrial Site Committee, that there remained unused some fifty-three prime industrial waterfront sites on other navigable channels within the state. It was likewise pointed out that all of these sites could be acquired for about what the proposed dam was estimated to cost.

Admittedly, the winning of approval for the Tellico Dam by TVA and area Congressmen pleased some people. Included were land speculators, landowners seeking large profits, local construction firms, and TVA employees seeking job security. "It is sad," said Peter D. Hollenbeck, an electronic engineer from nearby Huntsville, Alabama, member of the Tennessee Scenic Rivers Association, and an avid sport fisherman, "that there will always be those people who will readily destroy a priceless natural resource with total disregard for future generations in order to satisfy their own selfish desire."

Meanwhile, the TVA was busily advancing on the few remaining dam sites on the tributaries of the Tennessee. In the spring of 1966 it began construction on Tims Fork Dam which will eliminate forty miles of the scenic Elk River, once favored by canoeists and smallmouth bass fisherman. The big agency had chosen sites for two dams on the Duck River, at Columbia and Normandy, Tennessee. The Buffalo River, under study for wild river status has so far escaped.

In 1967, Congressman John D. Dingle of Michigan, long an effective voice in conservation matters, introduced his environmental quality act with the warning that, ". . . uncontrolled industrialization and urbanization . . . has brought mankind to the very brink of disaster.

"We have misused and eroded our land and allowed our waste to pollute and destroy rivers and streams, our lakes, our estuarine areas, and, in fact, the very oceans themselves . . . We have permitted the beauties of nature to be despoiled by unsightly roadways . . . Our cities and suburban areas too often have grown without plan or logical purpose . . . The time has come to take . . . action. . . ."

To accomplish this end, his bill, if passed, would have created a three-man Council on Environmental Quality, to study environmental information of all kinds and recommend direction of national policy for improving the quality of the environment.

What might well be required at this late date is a Board of Planners and Ecologists that could go a step further than advise and recommend. To insure the wisest permanent use of our remaining natural landscape calls for establishing an agency strong enough to tell the dam builders where they may and may not build, the highway planners what they must leave untouched, and the private landowners what they, as temporary stewards of the land, must not destroy permanently. Its name matters less than its legal authority and the quality of the scientists chosen to fill the chairs. If permitted only to advise and recommend, it will probably accomplish little.

Somewhere in the structure of the federal government there deserves to be an independent agency specializing in computing the benefit-cost ratios for proposed government projects, whether highways, dams, canals, or irrigation systems. In a system where each building agency is permitted to place a dollar value on the benefits to come from its own good works, objectivity is elusive. The Bureau of the Budget would no doubt insist that it fills this watchdog role, but though it checks the calculations of the building agencies, it does not draw up the original benefit-cost figures.

This Bureau has become the final authority in deciding the fate of numerous projects vital to the nation's resources. Who was it that finally decided that Walt Disney Productions would gain government permission to build a massive year-around recreational complex within the Sequoia National Forest in California? The proposal called for a newly modernized highway for eleven miles through Sequoia National Park, at public expense. Conservationists objected to this development of the remote Mineral King area on the basis that it could not avoid damaging the National Forest as well as the National Park, and pointed out that both the proposed roadwork within the park and the anchoring of ski-lift towers within the National Park violated Park Service rules.

The Secretary of the Department of Agriculture

Orville L. Freeman favored the development. Secretary Stewart L. Udall of the Department of the Interior along with George Hartzog, Director of the National Park Service protested it, but the plan went through. And the agency making the final decision was neither of these agencies, but the Bureau of the Budget.

In fairness to the Corps of Engineers, it must be admitted that its Board of Rivers and Harbors rejects about half of the congressionally suggested projects as economically unsound. But we have not yet created the non-partisan governmental machinery which can assign priority or test the national economic worth of proposed structures.

Changes of such magnitude are not easily attained. There are, however, some faster temporary ways which aroused voters could urge their Congressmen to employ. Laws or letters of agreement which say that the building and digging agencies must "consider" the findings of the Department of the Interior on proposed projects should be changed to give Interior actual veto power over extension of highways through its lands, dredging and filling of the estuaries, and the location of dams and other water control structures in areas where they might harm natural resources.

One quick way to slow the bulldozers is to cut budgets. It is not unreasonable to believe that the Corps budget could be safely cut by at least 30 per cent, and perhaps more, and still permit the engineers to perform the truly essential services. Perhaps the cuts might best be used in a sliding scale over a period of years to permit completion of projects already begun. Some projects still in their early stages could and should be stopped.

In 1964 Senator William Proxmire of Wisconsin, a former businessman, surveyed 380 dams and reservoir projects being built by the Corps and the Bureau of

Reclamation. Their total cost upon completion was to be $16 billion. How many of these projects, the Senator wanted to know, could be justified under normal business procedures? His study of the records produced a rule of thumb. Any project promising to return less than two dollars for each dollar spent, he found, was predestined to end up losing money. Only 160 of the 380 passed his exam. The estimated cost of the 220 others was $7½ billion.

Congress could grant the President the power of an item veto as he considers the annual rivers and harbors bills. As the pork barrel procedure now exists, the bill comes to the President's desk all tied up by the committee in a take-it or leave-it bundle of goodies. To veto one item in the long list, the President has to veto them all.

One President who was willing to veto the entire package was Chester A. Arthur. In 1882 he wrote a message on the subject, and its contents might well be recommended reading to federal servants in these times as well. "Appropriations of this nature, to be diverted peculiarly to local projects, tend to increase in number and amount." Pointing out that the citizens of each state, seeing other states gain federal money grants, would rush to gain their own share, the President added, "Thus as the bill becomes more objectionable it secures more support." The appropriations for rivers and harbors improvements, said the President, had increased year by year out of all proportions to the progress of the country. He questioned the constitutional basis for using federal money for strictly local improvements. But Congress passed its bill over his veto.

Another suggested change in legislation is an automatic expiration date for the congressional authorization granted a water management project. As it stands now, once a dam or waterway project is authorized it tends to remain authorized and rarely does the Corps request that Congress deauthorize one of its projects. But if it were to expire automatically within six or seven years unless work was begun, it might have to meet new and updated tests and not simply be an ace in the hole available to the builders at some distant time when conditions seem right for its resurrection.

Still another break on the pell-mell rush to dam the last of the free-flowing streams would be a cost-sharing plan requiring local agencies to contribute more of the money for water management projects. This would certainly gain a more critical study locally of the benefit-cost ratio for proposed dam-building projects. Much of the allure of the giant construction plan— the great sums of federal money being poured into local economies—would be diminished.

Neither the dam builders nor the highway planners like to hear suggestions that they consider alternate sites for their proposed projects. The usual procedure is for the Engineers to select the site, then go ahead with their costly and detailed planning, presenting it finally to laymen who must judge it without the benefit of other plans against which to compare it.

To be sure, the detailed planning that precedes the construction of such a public work is a costly item. It might well be, however, in view of the rapidly disappearing landscape that funds for equally detailed planning of alternate routes would be the best spent money of all.

There has never been an adequate inventory of the natural areas worthy of preservation. Such an inventory of scenic, ecological, and historical points of interest should begin with local organizations. The wetlands, patches of native prairie, ecologically important timberlands, streams, or unique parks and preserves could be described and catalogued at state and national level. Instead of running along behind the builders and diggers snapping at the Engineers' heels, the conservation minded could elevate themselves to leadership status. A soundly planned, complete inventory of important natural areas would be a step in this direction.

We have a challenge to hand down to future generations—a rich, productive, and beautiful land. The fight toward this end is not obstructionism, but we must put tomorrow in the limelight. A people blessed with a land of wealth and beauty should not pass on ugliness and desolation. The future does not deserve this heritage which we would hand it. We do not own the earth, not even our own acre of it, but only walk here at this instant which will become history.

Selected Bibliography

Anon.

1950. *A Water Policy for the American People*. Vol. 1, The President's Water Resources Policy Commission. U. S. Government Printing Office.

1901. Proceedings, Rampart Economic Advisory Board. First Conference, May 27-29, Elmendorf Air Force Base, Alaska.

1962. Second Conference, Jan. 10-12, Portland, Oregon. Third Conference, Mar. 30-31, Elmendorf Air Force Base, Alaska.

1963. *An Appraisal of Coal Strip Mining*, Tennessee Valley Authority, 13 pp.

1964. Proceedings, Conference on Surface Mining. June

1964, (mimeo) 64 pp. Council State Governments, Roanoke, Va.

1964. *Strip Mine Reclamation* (a digest). U. S. Department of Agriculture, 69 pp.

1964. *National Power Survey*. Report by the Federal Power Commission, U. S. Government Printing Office, 296 pp.

1964. Guides to Efficient Strip Mining. *Coal Age*, July, pp. 202-221.

1964. A Symposium on Strip Mine Reclamation, Wooster, Ohio, Vol. 64, No. 2, March 1964. *The Ohio Journal of Science*, The Ohio State University.

1965. *Lake Powell, Jewel of the Colorado*. Bureau of Reclamation, U. S. Department of the Interior.

1965. Proceedings of the Symposium on Strip Mine

Reclamation, Kentucky Department of Natural Resources, June, 47 pp.

1966. *The Third Wave.* U. S. Department of the Interior, 128 pp.

1966. *A Proposed Program for Scenic Roads and Parkways,* U. S. Department of Commerce, 254 pp.

1966. *The Population Challenge,* U. S. Department of the Interior, 80 pp.

1966. *Study of Strip and Surface Mining in Appalachia.* Strip and Surface Mine Study Policy Committee, U. S. Department of the Interior, 78 pp.

1966. Annual Report, Chief of Engineers. U. S. Army Civil Works Activities, Department of the Army Corps of Engineers, Vol. 1, 206 pp., and Vol. 2, 1845 pp., plus corresponding reports for earlier fiscal years.

1966. *Highways and Human Values.* Annual Report, 1966, Bureau of Public Roads, U. S. Department of Commerce, 72 pp.

1966. *Highway Statistics,* 1966. U. S. Department of Transportation, Washington, D.C., 186 pp.

1966. *Geneses of the Corps of Engineers.* The U. S. Army Corps of Engineers Museum, Fort Belvoir, Virginia.

1967. *Highway Statistics,* Summary to 1965, U. S. Department of Transportation, Mar., 179 pp.

1967. *Surface Mining and Our Environment,* U. S. Department of the Interior, 124 pp.

1967. *Water Resources Development by U. S. Army Corps of Engineers in Florida,* 93 pp. Maps. (Similar individual reports for each state.)

1967. *The Potomac.* The Report of the Potomac Planning Task Force, U. S. Government Printing Office, 103 pp.

1967. *Alaska Natural Resources and the Rampart Project,* U. S. Department of the Interior, 44 pp.

1967. *Cross-Florida Barge Canal Pre-Impoundment Studies.* Federal Water Pollution Control Administration, U. S. Department of the Interior, 37 pp.

1968. *National Highway Needs Report.* Department of Transportation, U. S. Government Printing Office, Washington, D.C., 66 pp.

Undated Taxation of Income from Natural Resources. The Federal Revenue System: Facts and Problems, A Report of Joint Congressional Committee on the Federal Revenue System, pp. 35-46.

AVERITT, P. Coal Reserves of the United States—A Progress Report. *U. S. Geological Survey Bulletin 1136.* 116 pp., 1961.

BARDACH, J. E. *Downstream: A Natural History of the River.* Harper & Row, New York, 278 pp., 1964.

BENNETT, G. V. *Grant to Eisenhower, Political Giveaways Unlimited.* Comet Press, New York, 134 pp., 1956.

BRIGGS, P. *Water—The Vital Essence.* Harper & Row, New York, 223 pp., 1967.

BROOKS, D. B. Strip Mine Reclamation and Economic Analysis. *Natural Resources Journal.* Vol. 6, No. 1, Jan. 1966, pp. 13-44.

BULLARD, O. *Crisis On the Columbia.* The Touchstone Press, Portland, Oregon, 146 pp., 1968.

CAUDILL, H. M. *Night Comes to the Cumberlands.* Little, Brown & Co., Boston, Mass., 394 pp., 1963.

CLAWSON, M. *Land for Americans.* Rand McNally, Chicago, 141 pp., 1963.

DASMANN, R. F. *The Last Horizon.* The Macmillan Co., New York, 279 pp., 1963.
The Destruction of California. The Macmillan Co., New York, 247 pp., 1965.

DICKEY, D. D. *The Little Tennessee River As an Economic Resource.* Industrial Development Institute, The Univ. of Oklahoma, Norman, Okla., (mimeo) 20 pp., 1964.

ECKSTEIN, O. *Water—Resources Development, The Economics of Project Evaluation,* Harvard Univ. Press, Cambridge, Mass., 290 pp., 1958.

FRYE, O. E., JR. *Remarks on the Fresh Water Fishery Resources of the St. Johns River Basin.* Florida Game and Fresh Water Fish Commission, (mimeo) 1968.

GENTILE, T. Maximum Recovery with Strip and Auger Equipment. *Mining Congress Journal,* Vol. 48, No. 8, Aug. 1962, pp. 65-67.

HALEY, W. A. and DOWD, J. J. *The Use of Augers In Surface Mining Bituminous Coal.* U. S. Bureau of Mines,

Report of Investigations 5325, 1957.

HART, H. C. *The Dark Missouri.* The University of Wisconsin Press, 260 pp., 1957.

HAVEMAN, R. H. *Water Resource Investment and the Public Interest,* Vanderbilt University Press, Nashville, Tenn., 1965.

HIRSHLEIFER, J. et al. *Water Supply, Economics, Technology and Policy.* The University of Chicago Press, 378 pp., 1960.

HODGE, F. W. The Cross-Florida Barge Canal. *Business and Economic Dimension,* July 1965, Bureau of Economic and Business Research, University of Florida, Gainesville.

HOLLINGSWORTH, J. A., JR. *History of Development of Strip Mining Machines,* Bucyrus-Erie Co., Milwaukee, Wis., 16 pp.

JACKSON, D., JR. Strip Mining, Reclamation, and the Public. *Coal Age,* Vol. 68, No. 5, May 1963, pp. 84-95.

KERR, R. S. *Land, Wood, and Water.* Fleet Publishing Co., New York, 380 pp. 1960.

KINNEY, E. C. *Extent of Acid Mine Pollution in the United States Affecting Fish and Wildlife.* U. S. Bureau Sport Fisheries and Wildlife Circ. 191, 1964, 27 pp.

LANDSBERG, H. H. *Natural Resources for U. S. Growth.* Johns Hopkins Press, Baltimore, Md., 1964.

LAUSCHE, F. J. U. S. Senator, Strip Coal Mining, *Congressional Record,* Vol. 110, No. 144, 1964.

LEOPOLD, A. S. and LEONARD, J. W. Effects of the Proposed Rampart Dam on Wildlife and Fisheries. *Transactions Thirty-First North American Wildlife and Natural Resources Conference,* pp. 454-59.

MEINERS, R. G. Strip Mining Legislation, *Natural Resources Journal,* Jan. 1964.

MERRILL, M. H. *The Public's Concern with the Fuel Minerals,* Thomas Law Book Co., St. Louis, Mo., 129 pp., 1960.

METCALF, L. Streams and Highways Use and Misuse of Public Resources. *Sierra Club Bull.,* Jan. 1964, p. 4.

MONTGOMERY, H. B. Conscientious Coal Stripping. *Coal Age,* Vol. 67, No. 7, July 1962, pp. 84-88.

MONTGOMERY, R. *Strip Mining in Kentucky.* The Kentucky Department of Natural Resources, 1965, 56 pp.

MOORE, J. R., Ed. *The Economic Impact of TVA.* The

Univ. of Tennessee Press, Knoxville, Tenn., 163 pp., 1967.

MOREELL, B. *Our Nation's Water Resources, Policies and Politics*. The University of Chicago, Chicago, Ill., 266 pp., 1957.

MORRIS, H. L. *The Plight of the Bituminous Coal Miner*. Univ. of Pennsylvania Press, Philadelphia, Pa., 1934.

MURRAY, T. J. The Investment Nobody Knows About. *Dun's Review*, April 1965, p. 40, 1965.

NEUZIL, D. R. Uses and Abuses of Highway Benefit-Cost Analysis. *Sierra Club Bulletin*, Jan. 1968, pp. 16-21.

SPURR, S. H. Rampart Dam: A Costly Gamble, *Audubon Magazine*, Vol. 68, No. 3, May-June 1966, p. 173.
Alaska's Economic Rampart, *Transactions Thirty-First North American Wildlife and Natural Resources Conference*, pp. 248-53, 1966.

SILCOX, F. A. *Scientific Aspects of Flood Control*. Symposium, Ecological Society of America, Rochester, New York, 47 pp., 1936.

SMITHIES, A. *The Budgetary Process in the United States*. McGraw-Hill Book Co., Inc., New York, 473 pp., 1955.

TABB, D. C. *Summary of Information on the Marine Ecology of the Florida Everglades Region in Relation to Fresh-Water Needs of Everglades National Park*. Institute of Marine Science, University of Miami, 1963.

THORNE, W., Ed. *Land and Water Use Symposium*. Pub. No. 73, American Association for the Advancement of Science, Washington, D.C., 362 pp., 1963.

WALSH, J. Strip Mining: Kentucky Begins to Close the Reclamation Gap. *Science*, Vol. 150, No. 3692, October 1965, pp. 35-39.

WING, W. G. The Concrete Juggernaut. *Audubon Magazine*, Vol. 68, No. 4, July-Aug. 1900, pp. 266-72.
What To Do Before The Highway Comes, *Audubon Magazine*, Vol. 68, No. 5, Sept-Oct. 1966, pp. 360-67.

YOUNG, W. H. and ANDERSON, R. L. Coal—Bituminous and Lignite. U. S. Bureau of Mines, *Minerals Yearbook 1964*, Vol. 2, pp. 41-161, 1965.

Index

ABOUT THE NATIONAL AUDUBON SOCIETY

Reflecting broadening perspectives and deepening concern about the dangers to the environment, the Audubon Society adopted a restatement of their objectives: *To promote the conservation of wildlife and the natural environment, and to educate man regarding his relationship with, and his place within, the natural environment as an ecological system.* Action and education, not appreciation and enjoyment of nature alone.

Audubon is the magazine of the Society. It is published bimonthly—and has been for 71 years. *Audubon's* field editors and contributors await assignment to any conservation battlefield in the world. No despoiler is above concern —neither biggest government nor biggest business.

A $10 individual membership in the National Audubon Society brings you six issues of *Audubon.* You will in turn be supporting the Society's broad program of conservation education and environmental action. You will be making a commitment to a cause—the Audubon cause, and yours as well.

National Audubon Society
1130 Fifth Avenue
New York, N.Y. 10028

I would like to receive a year's six issues of *Audubon,* and to support, through my annual membership, the programs of the society.

I prefer: ☐ a $10 individual membership
☐ a $12.50 family membership

Name:

Address:

City: State: Zip:

☐ I have enclosed my check or money order.
☐ Please send me a bill.